# 15-Minute Meals for 1 or 2
## Lou Seibert Pappas

Bristol Publishing Enterprises
San Leandro, California

# A Nitty Gritty® Cookbook

Printed in the United States of America.

ISBN 1-55867-028-9

Library of Congress Catalog Card Number
91-075893

Cover design: Frank Paredes
Cover photography:
  Food, Kathryn Opp
  Author, Renee Lynn
Food stylist: Carol Cooper Ladd
Illustrator: Kathleen Patterson-Estes

# CONTENTS

# SERVE CREATIVE, EASY, NUTRITIOUS MEALS WITH NITTY GRITTY® COOKBOOKS

Waffles
The Coffee Book
The Bread Machine Cookbook
The Bread Machine Cookbook II
The Bread Machine Cookbook III
The Bread Machine Cookbook IV
The Sandwich Maker Cookbook
The Juicer Book
Bread Baking (traditional),
    revised
The Kid's Cookbook, revised
The Kid's Microwave Cookbook
15-Minute Meals for 1 or 2
Recipes for the 9x13 Pan
Turkey, the Magic Ingredient
Chocolate Cherry Tortes and
    Other Lowfat Delights

Lowfat American Favorites
Lowfat International Cuisine
The Hunk Cookbook
Now That's Italian!
Fabulous Fiber Cookery
Low Salt, Low Sugar, Low Fat
    Desserts
What's for Breakfast?
Healthy Cooking on the Run
Healthy Snacks for Kids
Creative Soups & Salads
Quick & Easy Pasta Recipes,
    revised
Muffins, Nut Breads and More
The Barbecue Book
The Wok
New Ways with Your Wok

Quiche & Soufflé Cookbook
Easy Microwave Cooking
Cooking for 1 or 2
Meals in Minutes
New Ways to Enjoy Chicken
Favorite Seafood Recipes
No Salt, No Sugar, No Fat
    Cookbook
New International Fondue
    Cookbook
Extra-Special Crockery Pot
    Recipes
Favorite Cookie Recipes
Authentic Mexican Cooking
Fisherman's Wharf Cookbook
The Creative Lunch Box

Write or call for our free catalog.
Bristol Publishing Enterprises, Inc.
P.O. Box 1737, San Leandro, CA 94577
(800)346-4889; in California (510)895-4461

# 15-MINUTE MEALS FOR 1 OR 2

On a daily basis, fast and fresh are keynotes of today's cooking pattern for the nineties. When cooking for one and two, speed is of the essence and ultra-fresh ingredients, punctuated with herbs and ethnic seasonings, are essentials.

A smart way to solve the everyday culinary routine is to integrate the microwave with conventional cooking. Utilize the microwave for what it does best and simultaneously zero in on the oven, grill or stovetop to complete the meal.

Think of it as "tandem cooking." While the entrée broils or grills, let the microwave handle the vegetables. Meanwhile, toss a salad and embellish in a varying style. This way everything is ready simultaneously, clean-up is cut to a minimum and timing is swift.

The microwave does excel in cooking some foods and masters certain culinary techniques supremely well. It stars in cooking vegetables, fish, and poultry, and surpasses other methods when it comes to such tasks as melting chocolate, caramelizing sugar and toasting nuts.

By contrast other appliances perform far better for searing meats and baking to give a wonderful toasty, caramelized flavor and sometimes a desirable crispy crust. Rice, pasta and beans cook more evenly and usually just as fast conventionally so that method is certainly preferable to tying up the microwave. By using the microwave and other methods wisely the results can be gratifying.

On some occasions, let the microwave alone handle some imaginative, almost-instant platter dinners. This means a delectable "dinner on a plate" is ready in close to 10 minutes with three or four vegetables, a fruit accent and a flavor-packed lowfat gourmet sausage, fish fillet, or chicken or turkey breast strips. What's more, there is no clean-up and the warm plate means dinner stays piping hot.

Here is a collection of recipes showcasing ways to cook fast with a flavor flourish. Dinner can be set forth with ease in 15 to 20 minutes. What's more, the dishes are "heart healthy," lean in fat and high in zestful goodness. Enjoy the benefits of a neatly packaged format for setting forth succulent daily fare with ease.

## Nutritional Analysis
Recipes have been analyzed with *The Food Processor II* program from ESHA Research. Sodium has not been analyzed for some recipes when sodium content of an ingredient is unknown, for example chicken or fish stock.

# MICROWAVE HINTS

Good cooks are adept with conventional cooking techniques, but it pays to review some good principles of microwave cookery. The microwave is particularly ideal when cooking for one or two. Timing is ultra fast; whereas unlike conventional cooking, microwave timing is often doubled as portion size is doubled.

Certainly timing is a most critical factor in microwave cookery. An extra few seconds can make the difference between perfection and overcooking. It is far better to plan to set the timer to undercook, and then continue cooking to finish the dish if necessary, than to overcook in the beginning.

Not all ovens cook alike and power differs from one part of the country to another and at different times of day. Get to know your own particular oven. Some models require frequent turning or rotating of a dish for even cooking; for others, especially newer ones, it's not necessary. Testing was done in a late model microwave that cooked evenly; often the timing was faster than suggested in many published microwave books.

Remember to look while you cook. This way you can gauge if the chicken is turning opaque, the sugar is caramelizing golden brown, and the liquid is steaming. You can stop the cooking immediately by opening the oven door, but remember the food will continue to "coast cook."

Microwaves create heat by friction. Microwaves are attracted by water, fat and sugar. Positive particles in food molecules are attracted to the negative direction of the microwave. Microwaves reverse direction 2,450,000,000 times a second. Friction between molecules vibrating at almost 2½ billion times a second produces heat in food.

Microwaves penetrate food from all directions to a depth of ¾ to 1½ inches. Vibration causes heat in these areas and heat spreads through conduction to other parts of food as in conventional cooking. This is why it is best to cut chicken, turkey or fish in uniform size pieces or thicknesses.

Containers used must be nonmetal-glassware, ceramic casseroles, and dishwasher-safe plastic containers. Paper is all right for brief reheating. Circular and flat is the best shape for even, efficient microwaving. For these recipes, pie plates, measuring cups, soufflé dishes and custard cups suffice.

Follow recipe directions for covering the food. In most cases it is covered with plastic wrap, a lid, waxed paper or paper towels. Plastic wrap achieves a moist steamed result and the wrap should be vented. A casserole lid provides similar results. Waxed paper retains moisture without steam and avoids spattering. Paper towels absorb fat, moisture and steam and help prevent sogginess.

A few techniques ensure good results. For even cooking, foods with thicker denser portions should be arranged toward the outside edges of a dish. Try this with chicken drumsticks, fish steaks, asparagus spears, broccoli florets or an assortment of vegetables. When cooking or defrosting large, unevenly shaped foods such as whole chicken or fish fillets, small strips of aluminum foil can be used to prevent overcooking. Stirring encourages even cooking; always stir from the outside toward the center.

With fresh, zestful seasonings, the following recipes yield delicious dining. The real joy is their speed and ease. They are uncomplicated with natural juices utilized for entrée sauces. The many varied platter dinners can provide a change of menu for several weeks. Those who have used a microwave only for reheating, will find these platter dinners a joy, a revelation. The vegetable combinations make delicious accompaniments to broiled or barbecued fish, poultry or chicken. Many can also stand on their own for vegetarian-style dinners.

The fast appetizers, almost instant soups and colorful pizzas and pastas are other dining options. For quick desserts, warm fruits or a sundae are ideal.

Enjoy the ease of swift microwave preparation with excellent results because this is an *honest* approach to microwave cooking, meant to be used in tandem with the conventional style. What's more, microwave cookery is practically no-fat cookery, and through its speed, the vitamins and minerals are preserved.

# APPETIZERS

# CHILE CON QUESO

*This popular Mexican appetizer is easily doubled or tripled for a party occasion.*

¼ cup chopped yellow onion
1 jalapeño pepper, peeled and chopped
1 clove garlic, minced
2 tsp. olive oil

½ cup chopped, peeled tomatoes
¼ lb. Monterey Jack cheese
small hot tortilla chips

On a microwaveable serving plate, place onion, chile pepper, garlic and oil. Cover with waxed paper and microwave on High for 1 minute or until soft. Add tomatoes and microwave for 1 to 2 minutes to cook down and blend flavors, stirring once. Stir in cheese and microwave on Medium for 2 minutes or until melted, stirring once. Serve with a basket of hot tortilla chips.

**per serving without chips** 272 calories, 22 g fat (11 g saturated fat), 50 mg cholesterol, 15 g protein, 5 g carbohydrate, 360 mg sodium

# CRAB AND CHEESE NACHOS

Servings: 2

*Shrimp also works well in this zestful appetizer.*

1 cup tortilla chips
½ cup (2 oz.) shredded Monterey
  Jack cheese

¼ cup salsa or taco sauce
3 oz. crab meat or shrimp
1 green onion, chopped

Spread tortilla chips on a microwaveable platter and sprinkle with cheese. Spoon on salsa and sprinkle crab and onion over all. Cover with waxed paper and microwave on High for 1 minute or until cheese melts.

*per serving*   234 calories, 14 g fat (6 g saturated fat), 53 mg cholesterol, 17 g protein, 11 g carbohydrate, 371 mg sodium

# HOT CRAB AND PINE NUT DIP

*This is a fast dip to serve with water biscuits or celery sticks or dollop into raw mushroom caps.*

2 tbs. pine nuts or slivered almonds
6 oz. light cream cheese
2 tsp. balsamic vinegar
1 tsp. grated lemon zest
1 green onion, chopped

1 tbs. dry white wine
1 tsp. lemon juice
6 oz. crab meat, flaked
dash Tabasco to taste
crackers or celery or mushrooms

Sprinkle nuts on a pie plate. Microwave on High for 2 to 3 minutes or just until golden. In a bowl, microwave cream cheese on High for 30 seconds, just to soften. Mix in vinegar, lemon zest, onion, wine, lemon juice, crab meat and Tabasco. Spoon mixture into a 2-cup baking dish; cover with waxed paper and microwave on Medium High 2 to 3 minutes or until hot through, stirring once or twice. Sprinkle nuts over top. Serve with crackers, sticks of celery or mushroom caps.

For a festive presentation, spoon crab and cheese mixture into 2 red pepper half shells, cover with waxed paper, place on a pie plate, and microwave on Medium High for 2 to 3 minutes or until hot through.

*per ¼-cup serving*   177 calories, 14 g fat (8 g saturated fat), 60 mg cholesterol, 10 g protein, 2 g carbohydrate, 197 mg sodium

# CROSTINI

*In Florence you discover this appealing hot chicken liver appetizer in the ultra-popular cellar restaurants that serve excellent regional specialties.*

1 shallot, chopped
2 tsp. olive oil
1/4 lb. chicken livers, finely chopped
1 anchovy, chopped
1 tbs. dry Vermouth

1 tbs. shredded Parmesan cheese
1/2 tsp. fresh oregano, chopped or 1/8 tsp. dried
4 small rounds French bread, toasted and spread with garlic butter

In a small microwaveable dish, place shallot, oil, chicken livers, anchovy and Vermouth. Cover with waxed paper and microwave on Medium for 2 minutes or until livers lose their pink color. Mash with a fork and mix in cheese and oregano. Spread on hot rounds of toast.

***per serving*** 447 calories, 19 g fat (8 g saturated fat), 385 mg cholesterol, 23 g protein, 45 g carbohydrate, 649 mg sodium

# SPICY BEAN DIP

*This lively dip is great with chips as an appetizer or use any leftover dip as the basis for a hot tortilla salad.*

1 tsp. olive oil
1 clove garlic, minced
2 green onions, chopped
1 cup cooked or canned red kidney beans
½ cup chopped tomatoes or halved cherry tomatoes

1 tsp. chopped pickled jalapeño peppers or red peppers
dash Tabasco
½ cup shredded Monterey Jack cheese
2 tbs. chopped cilantro
tortilla chips or sliced jicama, turnip or fennel

In a 4-cup casserole combine oil, garlic and onion; microwave, uncovered, on High for 30 seconds. Stir in beans, tomatoes, peppers and Tabasco. Cover with vented plastic wrap and microwave on High for 2 to 3 minutes or until heated through. Mash with a potato masher, leaving a few coarse pieces. Sprinkle with cheese; microwave uncovered, at Medium for 1 to 2 minutes or until cheese has melted. Sprinkle with cilantro and serve with tortilla chips or raw vegetables.

*per ¼-cup serving*   85 calories, 4 g fat (2 g saturated fat), 8 mg cholesterol, 5 g protein, 8 g carbohydrate, 206 mg sodium

**Variation: FIESTA SALAD TORTILLA**    Servings: 2

two 6-inch flour tortillas
*Spicy Bean Dip*
1 cup shredded lettuce

½ avocado, sliced
2 tbs. sour cream or yogurt
cherry tomatoes for garnish

Wrap tortillas in a damp paper towel and microwave on high until softened, about 1 to 2 minutes. Spread about ⅓ cup *Spicy Bean Dip* over each tortilla. Sprinkle with shredded lettuce, top with avocado slices and dollop each with a tablespoon of sour cream or yogurt. Garnish with a few cherry tomatoes.

***per serving***   384 calories, 21 g fat (5 g saturated fat), 20 mg cholesterol, 14 g protein, 39 g carbohydrate, 555 mg sodium

# HOT PITA TRIANGLES

*These wholesome crispy bread triangles are great alone or with a dip. If they become cold, they easily reheat right in a wicker serving basket.*

1 whole wheat pita bread
2 tbs. olive oil
1 garlic clove, finely chopped

1 tsp. fresh oregano, chopped or ¼ tsp. dried
2 tbs. grated Parmesan cheese

Split pita bread in half horizontally and cut each piece into 6 triangles. Lay on a paper towel on a microwaveable plate. Place oil and garlic in a small bowl and microwave on High for 45 seconds or until hot. Spread on pita breads. Sprinkle with oregano and cheese. Microwave on High for 30 seconds to 1 minute or until cheese is melted. Makes 1 dozen.

***per serving***  235 calories, 16 g fat (3 g saturated fat), 5 mg cholesterol, 6 g protein, 18 g carbohydrate, 286 mg sodium

## Variation
Omit cheese and oregano; sprinkle with 2 tbs. toasted sesame seeds.

# STUFFED MUSHROOMS

Servings: 2

*These hot morsels are excellent as an appetizer or vegetable accompaniment.*

4 oz. button mushrooms
1 shallot, chopped
1 tbs. pesto or minced fresh basil or
    tarragon and Italian parsley

1 tbs. shredded Romano cheese
1 tbs. olive oil
2 tbs. dry white wine

Remove stems from mushrooms and chop. Place in a small microwaveable bowl with shallot. Cover with plastic wrap and microwave on High for 45 seconds to soften. Add pesto or herbs, sprinkle with cheese and spoon into mushroom caps. Place oil and wine in a microwaveable pie plate. Add mushrooms. Cover with waxed paper and microwave on High for 1 minute or until hot through and cheese is melted.

*per serving*   114 calories, 8 g fat (1 g saturated fat), 3 mg cholesterol, 3 g protein, 9 g carbohydrate, 36 mg sodium

# FRUIT-FILLED QUESADILLAS

*Mango or papaya slices make a refreshing accent in hot cheesy tortilla triangles.*

two 8-inch flour tortillas
½ cup shredded Monterey Jack or
  cheddar cheese
¼ cup slivered red pepper

1 green onion, chopped
4 thin slices of mango, papaya or
  nectarines

Place a tortilla on a paper towel on a microwaveable plate. Sprinkle with cheese, red pepper and onion; lay fruit slices over all. Top with second tortilla, pressing edges together. Cover with a paper towel. Microwave on High for 1 minute or until hot through and cheese is melted. Let stand 2 minutes. Cut into triangles.

Note: for a spicier accent, add 1 tbs. chopped green chile pepper on top of cheese.

*per serving*   260 calories, 12 g fat (6 g saturated fat), 25 mg cholesterol, 10 g protein, 32 g carbohydrate, 290 mg sodium

# FIVE SPICE TOASTED NUTS

*The exotic overtones of five spice permeate these crisp toasty nuts. Use any one nut or a combination. You can buy five spice on the Oriental food shelf at your grocery, or wherever Oriental groceries are sold.*

2 tsp. olive oil
1 tsp. balsamic vinegar
⅛ tsp. five spice
⅛ tsp. ground cinnamon

dash ground cloves
dash Tabasco
½ cup shelled whole pecans,
   almonds, hazelnuts or walnuts

In a 9-inch pie plate place oil, vinegar, five spice, cinnamon, cloves and Tabasco; stir to blend. Microwave on High 30 seconds. Add nuts, stir to coat, and microwave on High about 5 minutes, stirring twice, and cooking until toasty. Let cool. Store in a tightly sealed jar. Refrigerate to keep longer than 2 weeks.

---

**per ¼-cup serving**   222 calories, 23 g fat (2 g saturated fat), 0 mg cholesterol, 2 g protein, 5 g carbohydrate, 1 mg sodium

---

# EASY YOGURT CHEESE

¾ cup

*Either homemade yogurt or commercial yogurt prepared without gelatin can be used for this versatile, lowfat cheese. This makes a great topping on baked potatoes seasoned with chives, or blend it with garlic puree for another topping. It's good on toast with fruit preserves, or wherever you might normally use cream cheese.*

1 pint plain lowfat yogurt without gelatin

Using a colander lined with a double thickness of cheesecloth, or a regular cheesemaker strainer placed over a deep casserole or bowl, spoon in yogurt. Cover with plastic wrap and refrigerate about 24 hours or until as thick as desired. Scoop cheese into a container, cover and use in desired ways. Keeps refrigerated about 3 to 4 days. Discard liquid that remains.

***per ¼-cup serving*** 95 calories, 2 g fat (1.5 g saturated fat), 9 mg cholesterol, 8 g protein, 11 g carbohydrate, 106 mg sodium

# SALADS

WESTERN COBB SALAD. . . . . . . . . 19
CELERY VICTOR . . . . . . . . . 20
LEEK VICTOR . . . . . . . . . . 21
FENNEL VICTOR . . . . . . . . . 21
PINE NUT CHICORY SALAD . . . . . . 22
NEW POTATO AND SMOKED TUNA SALAD . . . 23
TOSSED SHREDDED CHICKEN SALAD . . . . 24
ISLAND CHICKEN AND PAPAYA SALAD . . . 26
WARM JICAMA AND TURKEY SALAD. . . . . 27
SPINACH AND HOT CHICKEN LIVER SALAD . . 28
MUSTARD VINAIGRETTE . . . . . . . 30

# WESTERN COBB SALAD

*The lively mingling of chicken, avocado, blue cheese and bacon makes this a robust full-meal salad plate.*

8 oz. boneless chicken or turkey
  breast
1 tbs. lemon juice
butter lettuce and watercress
2 tbs. *Mustard Vinaigrette*, page 30

6 cherry tomatoes, halved
½ avocado, peeled and cubed
¼ cup blue cheese, crumbled
3 strips crumbled, cooked bacon
2 hard-cooked eggs, diced (optional)

Place chicken in a 9-inch pie plate and drizzle with lemon juice. Cover with waxed paper and microwave on High for 1½ to 2 minutes or until cooked through. Chill. Tear into strips or cubes. Place greens on serving plates. Toss chicken in *Mustard Vinaigrette* and spoon on top.

Encircle with spokes of cherry tomatoes, avocado, cheese, bacon and eggs. Makes 2 servings.

Note: or use leftover roasted or poached chicken breast.

---

**per serving** 510 calories, 29 g fat (7 g saturated fat), 327 mg cholesterol, 51 g protein, 13 g carbohydrate, 544 mg sodium

# CELERY VICTOR

*This long-time classic salad works admirably in the microwave. Another time try it with leeks or fennel.*

1 small head celery hearts
¾ cup chicken broth
1 cup mixed greens, preferably with
  watercress

3 tbs. *Mustard Vinaigrette*, page 30
4 anchovy fillets for garnish

Remove any outer tough stalks of celery and cut off tops, making lengths about 5 to 6 inches from the base; cut into quarters. Place in a 1½-quart microwaveable casserole, add broth, cover and microwave on High for 5 to 6 minutes or until tender when pierced with a fork. Let cool in broth. Refrigerate. To serve, place greens on serving plates, divide celery hearts on top and spoon *Mustard Vinaigrette* over all. Garnish with anchovy fillets.

---

*per serving*   74 calories, 3 g fat (.5 g saturated fat), 7 mg cholesterol, 5 g protein, 9 g carbohydrate, 964 mg sodium

**Variations: LEEK VICTOR or FENNEL VICTOR**

Instead of celery hearts, substitute 4 small leeks, white part only, split lengthwise. Or, instead of celery hearts, substitute 1 stalk fennel, cut in ¾-inch thick lengthwise slices, using white part only.

# PINE NUT CHICORY SALAD

*A warm balsamic vinaigrette cloaks curly chicory for a sprightly salad. Chicory is sometimes called curly endive.*

about 2 cups torn chicory or romaine
  lettuce
1½ tbs. olive oil
1 tbs. balsamic vinegar
1 tsp. Dijon mustard

salt and pepper to taste
1 tsp. fresh chopped tarragon or ¼
  tsp. dried
1 shallot, chopped
2 tbs. toasted pine nuts or pistachios

Place chicory in a medium bowl. In a 1-cup glass measure, combine oil, vinegar, mustard, salt, pepper, tarragon, shallot and nuts. Microwave on High 30 seconds to 1 minute or until hot. Toss with chicory.

**per serving**   374 calories, 32 g fat (5 g saturated fat), 0 mg cholesterol, 14 g protein, 20 g carbohydrate, 120 mg sodium

# NEW POTATO AND SMOKED TUNA SALAD   Servings: 2

*The secret to this potato salad is to cook the spuds in their jackets and marinate them while still warm. Other smoked fish can substitute for canned smoked tuna.*

½ lb. small new potatoes
3 tbs. water
2 tbs. olive oil
1 tbs. white wine vinegar
1 tsp. Dijon mustard
1 tbs. each chopped Italian parsley
  and chives or green onion tops

1 can (6 or 7 oz.) smoked albacore
  tuna or other smoked fish, flaked in
  large pieces
1 tbs. capers
butter lettuce or red lettuce
½ cup red or gold cherry tomatoes

Pierce potatoes. Place them in a 1-quart casserole. Add water, cover tightly and cook on in a microwave on High for 3 to 4 minutes or until tender, turning them once. Let stand, covered, for 10 minutes. Drain, then slice ⅛-inch thick. In a bowl, place oil, vinegar, and mustard; add potatoes and toss to mix. Let marinate for 30 minutes. Stir in parsley, chives, tuna, and capers. Spoon onto greens and garnish with cherry tomatoes. For conventional cooking, cook potatoes in boiling salted water for 10 to 12 minutes or just until tender.

***per serving***   432 calories, 21 g fat (3 g saturated fat), 15 mg cholesterol, 29 g protein, 33 g carbohydrate, 350 mg sodium

# TOSSED SHREDDED CHICKEN SALAD

Servings: 2

*Sprightly Oriental seasonings uplift this chicken salad with its refreshing fruit accent.*

8 oz. boneless chicken breasts or
  turkey breast
1 tbs. lemon juice
1½ cups shredded cabbage or
  iceberg lettuce
2 green onions, chopped

3 tbs. chopped cilantro
¼ cup chopped jicama
*Oriental Dressing*, follows
 2 tbs. toasted sesame seeds (optional)
4 fresh pineapple spears or avocado slices

Place chicken breasts in a 9-inch pie plate. Drizzle with lemon juice. Cover with waxed paper and microwave on High for 2 minutes or until cooked through. Chill. Cut into ½-inch strips. In a bowl, place cabbage, onions, cilantro, jicama and chicken. Pour *Oriental Dressing* over salad and toss lightly. Spoon into serving bowls, such as shallow soup bowls, and garnish with sesame seeds and pineapple or avocado.

Note: or use leftover roasted or poached chicken or turkey breast.

## Oriental Dressing

¼ tsp. *each* dry mustard and grated lemon zest
1 tsp. *each* white wine vinegar, honey and soy sauce
1 tbs. *each* sesame oil, safflower oil and lemon or lime juice

Mix together in a small container.

*per serving*   327 calories, 11 g fat (2 g saturated fat), 96 mg cholesterol, 39 g protein, 19 g carbohydrate, 109 mg sodium

# ISLAND CHICKEN AND PAPAYA SALAD

Servings: 2

*Papaya half shells make pretty boats for a salad medley. If you can't find papaya, cantaloupe halves, cut zig-zag style, can also be used.*

8 oz. boneless chicken or turkey breast
1 tbs. lime juice
½ cup diced celery hearts or fennel
½ cup seedless grapes
*Chutney Dressing*, follows

a few butter lettuce leaves
1 small papaya, halved and seeded
  or 1 small cantaloupe
1½ tbs. chopped macadamia nuts or
  pistachios

Place chicken in a 9-inch pie plate and drizzle with lime juice. Cover with waxed paper and microwave on High for ½ to 2 minutes or until cooked through. Chill. Tear into strips or cubes. Place in a bowl with celery hearts and grapes. Add *Chutney Dressing* and mix lightly. Arrange greens on serving plates. Spoon salad into papaya halves. Place on greens and sprinkle with nuts. Note: or use leftover roasted or poached chicken or turkey breast.

## Chutney Dressing

2 tbs. *each* sour cream and yogurt
1½ tsp. *each* lime juice and thawed orange juice concentrate
1 tbs. apricot or mango chutney

Mix together in a bowl.

*per serving* 382 calories, 12 g fat (4 g saturated fat), 103 mg cholesterol, 38 g protein, 32 g carbohydrate, 142 mg sodium

# WARM JICAMA AND TURKEY SALAD

Servings: 2

*If you don't know about jicama, ask your grocer to show you this large root. It's delicious alone as a raw vegetable, or in stir-fries and in salads. This crunchy salad goes together in a flourish.*

2 cups mixed salad greens torn into bite-size pieces
½ cup red or gold pepper strips
½ cup julienned jicama
1 green onion, chopped
8 oz. turkey breast meat, cut in strips
2 tsp. sweet hot mustard
1 tsp. lemon juice
2 tbs. olive oil
1 small clove garlic, minced
2 tbs. balsamic vinegar
1 tsp. fresh chopped tarragon or ¼ tsp. dried
salt and pepper to taste
½ cup seedless grapes

Toss greens, pepper strips, jicama and onion in a large bowl. Place turkey in a pie plate and spread with a mixture of mustard and lemon juice; cover with waxed paper and microwave on High 1½ minutes. Let stand 2 minutes. In a small bowl, combine oil, garlic, vinegar, tarragon, salt and pepper; microwave on high for 10 to 20 seconds until just boiling. Place hot turkey on greens, pour hot vinaigrette over and toss gently to coat well. Arrange on serving plates and sprinkle with grapes.

*per serving*  350 calories, 16 g fat (2 g saturated fat), 97 mg cholesterol, 37 g protein, 16 g carbohydrate, 139 mg sodium

# SPINACH AND HOT CHICKEN LIVER SALAD

*Hot chicken livers dress up a spinach salad.*

4 chicken livers
1 tbs. sherry
1 bunch spinach, torn into bite-size
  pieces
2 tbs. olive oil
1 tbs. red wine vinegar

½ tbs. lemon juice
1 tsp. Dijon mustard
1 shallot, minced
1½ tbs. lightly toasted pine nuts or
  roasted sunflower seeds
freshly ground pepper to taste

Place livers around the outer edge of a 9-inch pie plate. Drizzle with sherry. Cover with waxed paper and microwave on Medium for 3 to 4 minutes or until barely cooked through. Let stand a few minutes. Place spinach in a large mixing bowl. In a small bowl combine oil, vinegar, lemon juice, mustard and shallot. Cover with waxed paper and microwave on High for 30 seconds. Pour over spinach and toss. Spoon onto serving plates. Top with livers and sprinkle with nuts. Season with freshly ground pepper.

**per serving** 262 calories, 19 g fat (3 g saturated fat), 252 mg cholesterol, 13 g protein, 10 g carbohydrate, 102 mg sodium

# MUSTARD VINAIGRETTE

*This dressing is excellent both for salads and cooked vegetables. It also makes a good coating on fish or chicken for microwaving.*

¼ cup olive oil
1 tbs. Dijon-style mustard
1½ tbs. red or white wine vinegar
2 tbs. dry white wine

2 shallots, chopped
1 tsp. fresh chopped tarragon or
  ¼ tsp. dried
dash salt and freshly ground pepper

In a small bowl, stir together oil and mustard to blend. Stir in vinegar, wine, shallots, tarragon, salt and pepper. Cover and chill until ready to use. If desired, for an emulsified dressing, blend in a blender or food processor. Makes approximately 4 servings.

**per serving**   20 calories, 1 g fat (0 g saturated fat), 0 mg cholesterol, .5 g protein, 3 g carbohydrate, 26 mg sodium

# SOUPS

# GINGERED CRAB BROTH

*Here's a fast soup to steep in minutes. Lemon grass makes a delightful addition when available.*

1 green onion, chopped
1 tsp. chopped parsley
½ tsp. chopped ginger root
½ tsp. chopped lemon zest or lemon
  grass (optional)

½ tsp. chopped tarragon or dill or
  ⅛ tsp. dried
1 mushroom, thinly sliced
6 oz. fish stock or mussel broth
1½ oz. crab meat

In a 1-pint container, place onion, parsley, ginger root, lemon zest or lemon grass, tarragon, mushrooms and broth. Cover with vented plastic wrap and microwave on High for 2 minutes. Add crab meat and microwave 30 seconds longer or until heated through. Makes 1 serving.

For 2 servings, double ingredients and use a 1-quart container. Microwave on High 3 to 4 minutes, add crab and microwave 1 minute longer.

---

*per serving* 158 calories, 3 g fat (0 g saturated fat), 28 mg cholesterol, 18 g protein, 14 g carbohydrate, — mg sodium

# CUCUMBER YOGURT SOUP

*This is a cooling starter for a summer day.*

1 large cucumber, peeled, seeded
  and chopped
2 green onions, chopped
1 clove garlic, minced
1 tsp. fresh dill
2 leaves mint, chopped

¾ cup chicken stock
1 tbs. white wine vinegar
⅓ cup lowfat yogurt
½ tsp. grated lemon zest
mint sprigs for garnish

In a large 1-quart casserole, combine cucumber, onions, garlic, dill, mint, stock and vinegar. Cover and microwave on High for about 3 to 4 minutes or until cucumbers are tender. Let stand 5 minutes. Then process in a blender or food processor until smooth. Chill. When ready to serve, stir in yogurt and lemon zest. Garnish with mint.

---

***per serving***   76 calories, 1 g fat (.5 g saturated fat), 2 mg cholesterol, 5 g protein, 10 g carbohydrate, — mg sodium

---

# ITALIAN VEGETABLE SOUP

Servings: 2

*Dried porcini mushrooms give an uplift to this wholesome soup.*

2 dried porcini or shiitake mushrooms,
  soaked in water 15 minutes
1 medium potato, peeled and chopped
1 carrot, peeled and chopped
1 leek, chopped

1 inner stalk celery, chopped
1 tsp. fresh thyme or ½ tsp. dried
1¼ cups chicken stock
¼ cup dry white wine
salt and pepper to taste

Reserve mushroom liquid and chop mushrooms. Place mushrooms and liquid in a 1-quart casserole with potato, carrot, leek, celery, thyme and stock. Cover and microwave on High for about 8 minutes, or until vegetables are tender. Let stand 5 minutes. Puree in a blender or food processor with wine and season with salt and pepper. Return to casserole and microwave covered just until hot through.

For conventional cooking, simmer soup in a saucepan for 15 to 20 minutes or until vegetables are tender. Puree in a blender.

---

***per serving***  221 calories, 1 g fat (0 g saturated fat), 0 mg cholesterol, 4 g protein, 27 g carbohydrate, — mg sodium

# JAMAICAN CARROT SOUP

Servings: 2

*Peanut butter gives an intriguing flavor to this creamy orange soup.*

1/3 cup chopped onion
1 clove garlic, minced
1 tsp. olive oil
3 medium carrots, peeled and diced
2 tsp. peanut butter
dash Tabasco

1 1/4 cups chicken stock
1/4 cup fruity white wine
yogurt for garnish
chopped peanuts or toasted sunflower
   seeds for garnish

Place onion, garlic and oil in a 1- quart casserole. Microwave on High for 1 minute or until onion is soft. Add carrots, peanut butter, Tabasco and stock. Cover and microwave on High for 5 to 6 minutes or until very tender. Let stand 5 minutes. Puree in a blender or food processor with wine. Return to casserole and microwave covered on High for 1 minute or just until hot through. Ladle into bowls; garnish with a dollop of yogurt and a sprinkling of nuts or seeds.

For conventional cooking, simmer soup in a saucepan for 15 minutes or until carrots are tender. Add wine and heat through. Puree in a blender, then ladle into bowls and garnish.

*per serving*   235 calories, 7 g fat (1 g saturated fat), 0 mg cholesterol, 4 g protein, 17 g carbohydrate, — mg sodium

# DUO MUSHROOM SOUP

Servings: 2

*Both fresh and dried mushrooms mingle in this appealing creamy soup.*

1/4 lb. mushrooms, chopped
1 tsp. olive oil
1½ cups chicken stock
1 dried porcini or shiitake mushroom,
  rinsed and cut into pieces
2 green onions, chopped
2 tbs. minced parsley

1 shallot, chopped
1 tsp. fresh tarragon or 1/4 tsp. dried
1/3 cup cooked brown rice
1/4 cup lowfat yogurt
1 tbs. dry sherry
thinly sliced mushrooms for garnish

Toss mushrooms and oil in a large casserole dish. Cover and microwave on High for 45 seconds, stirring. Add stock, mushroom pieces, onions, parsley, shallot and tarragon. Cover with vented plastic wrap and microwave on High for 4 minutes. Let stand 5 minutes. Pour mixture into a food processor or blender and process until smooth, adding rice, yogurt and sherry while motor is running. Serve immediately, garnished with mushroom slices.

---

***per serving*** 217 calories, 6 g fat (2 g saturated fat), 9 mg cholesterol, 12 g protein, 29 g carbohydrate, — mg sodium

# CURRIED GREEN PEA SOUP  Servings: 2

*This pretty pale green soup is excellent hot or cold.*

½ tsp. curry powder
1 tsp. olive oil
1 shallot, chopped
1 small leek, white part only, chopped
1 small potato, peeled and diced
1¼ cups chicken stock

1 cup fresh or frozen petite peas
salt and pepper to taste
¼ cup lowfat yogurt
¼ cup dry white wine
mint sprigs for garnish

In a large casserole place curry powder, oil, shallot and leek; turn to coat with oil. Cover and microwave on High for 45 seconds; stir. Add potato and stock. Cover and microwave on High until potato is almost tender, about 5 minutes. Add peas and microwave 2 minutes longer. Let stand 5 minutes. Transfer to a food processor or blender and process until smooth. Blend in salt, pepper, yogurt and wine. Serve immediately or refrigerate and serve chilled. Or reheat in a microwave on Medium for 2 or 3 minutes or until hot through. Serve in bowls garnished with mint.

*per serving* 205 calories, 4 g fat (1 g saturated fat), 2 mg cholesterol, 8 g protein, 31 g carbohydrate, — mg sodium

# WATERCRESS PESTO BROTH

*A spoonful of watercress pesto, redolent of Parmesan, uplifts this wine-laced broth.*

1 tsp. olive oil
2 tbs. grated Parmesan or Romano
  cheese
½ clove garlic, minced

2 tbs. chopped fresh watercress or
  fresh basil
1½ cups beef broth
¼ cup dry red wine

In a small bowl, mix together oil, cheese, garlic and watercress. Combine broth and wine; pour into 2 microwaveable mugs. Cover with vented plastic wrap and microwave on High for 1 minute and 45 seconds or until heated through. Dollop with a spoonful of pesto.

*per serving*   161 calories, 4 g fat (2 g saturated fat), 5 mg cholesterol, 4 g protein, 4 g carbohydrate, — mg sodium

# MEXICAN RANCHERO SOUP

Servings: 1 or 2

*This colorful soup makes a nice starter for a South-of-the-Border menu.*

2 cups chicken stock
dash Tabasco
¼ cup slivered chicken or boiled ham
  or prosciutto
1 green onion, chopped

2 cherry tomatoes, chopped
3 tbs. chopped cilantro
¼ cup diced avocado
1 tbs. roasted pumpkin seeds
tortilla chips for accompaniment

In a 1-quart casserole combine stock, Tabasco, chicken and onion. Cover with vented plastic wrap and microwave on High until hot through, about 3 minutes. Add tomatoes, cilantro, avocado and pumpkin seeds; ladle into bowls. Accompany with tortilla chips.

For 1 serving, divide ingredients in half and microwave in a large mug for about 1½ to 2 minutes.

For conventional cooking, heat soup ingredients in a saucepan until hot through.

*per serving*   141 calories, 10 g fat (2 g saturated fat), 15 mg cholesterol, 8 g protein, 7 g carbohydrate, — mg sodium

# THAI LEMON GRASS SOUP

*Clean, scintillating flavors uplift the taste buds in this delightful fast Far East soup.*

1½ cups chicken stock
1 tsp. light soy sauce
dash Tabasco
1 tsp. finely diced lemon grass or
   grated lemon zest

2 tsp. chopped fresh basil
1½ tsp. chopped fresh mint
6 medium raw shrimp, peeled and
   halved vertically
2 green onions, finely chopped

In a 1-quart casserole, combine stock, soy sauce, Tabasco, lemon grass, basil and mint. Cover and microwave on High until heated through, about 4 to 5 minutes. Arrange shrimp around sides of a pie plate. Cover with vented plastic wrap and microwave on High for 45 seconds to 1 minute or until shrimp turn pink. Add shrimp and onions to soup and serve hot. Makes 2 servings.

For conventional cooking, simmer chicken stock with seasonings in a saucepan for 10 minutes. Add shrimp and simmer until shrimp turn pink, about 3 to 4 minutes. Add onions just before serving.

*per serving*  56 calories, 1 g fat (0 g saturated fat), 55 mg cholesterol, 8 g protein, 4 g carbohydrate, — mg sodium

# BLACK BEAN SOUP IN PUMPKIN SHELLS

Servings: 2

*The petite tiny pumpkins make neat edible containers for a bean soup. For a shortcut, use canned beans.*

2 small 5-inch pumpkins
1½ cups cooked black turtle beans
  or kidney beans, drained
⅓ cup lowfat yogurt
2 tbs. lime or lemon juice

dash Tabasco
1 tbs. sherry
3 tbs. chopped cilantro
½ cup chicken stock, approximate
cilantro sprigs for garnish

Cut tops from pumpkins and scoop out seeds. Place in a large casserole; add ¼ cup water. Cover and microwave on High for about 6 to 8 minutes or until almost tender. Let stand 5 minutes. In a blender, puree cooked beans, yogurt, lime juice, Tabasco, sherry, chopped cilantro and enough stock to make a soupy consistency. Spoon into pumpkin shells. Replace lids. Place in a 9-inch pie plate and cover with waxed paper. Microwave on High for 2 to 3 minutes or until hot through. Serve garnished with cilantro sprigs encircling each pumpkin shell.

*per serving* 273 calories, 2 g fat (1 g saturated fat), 2 mg cholesterol, 15 g protein, 51 g carbohydrate, — mg sodium

# VEGETABLE SIDE DISHES AND ENTRÉES

# FETTUCINE WITH ARTICHOKES

Servings: 2

*For fun accompany this fast pasta entrée with bread sticks wrapped with prosciutto and a mixed greens salad with red and gold cherry tomatoes.*

6 oz. fettucine, cooked according to
    package directions
2 tbs. olive oil
1 shallot, chopped
1 (10 oz.) package artichoke hearts,
    thawed and halved

¼ cup chopped red bell pepper
½ cup heavy cream
½ cup grated Parmesan cheese
freshly ground pepper to taste
2 tbs. chopped Italian parsley

While pasta cooks, place oil, shallots, artichoke hearts, peppers and cream in a 2-quart casserole. Microwave on High for 3 to 4 minutes or until artichokes are almost tender. Add cheese and microwave on Medium for 1 minute or until melted. Cook pasta, drain and add to sauce, tossing to coat. Season with pepper. Sprinkle with parsley.

---

*per serving*  645 calories, 44 g fat (20 g saturated fat), 101 mg cholesterol, 20 g protein, 47 g carbohydrate, 671 mg sodium

# ARTICHOKES WITH VEGETABLE MELANGE

Servings: 2

*The extra moisture of the juices enhances artichokes as they steam to tenderness.*

2 artichokes
½ lemon
2 tsp. olive oil
1 clove garlic, minced
1 small onion, chopped

1 small carrot, peeled and shredded
¼ cup chicken stock
1 tbs. chopped parsley
1½ tsp. lemon juice

Cut off stems and about ¾ inch from tops of artichokes. Pull off tough bottom leaves and with scissors snip off points of outer leaves. Rub outsides of artichokes with cut side of lemon. In a 1½-quart casserole, combine oil, garlic, onion and carrot. Cover tightly and microwave on High for 3 minutes or until vegetables are soft. Stir in stock, parsley and lemon juice. Position artichokes stem side down on top of vegetables. Cover tightly and cook on high for about 8 minutes or until bases pierce easily, rotating dish twice. Let stand 5 minutes. Serve artichokes with vegetables; spoon juices over all.

*per serving*   139 calories, 5 g fat (1 g saturated fat), 1 mg cholesterol, 6 g protein, 21 g carbohydrate, 257 mg sodium

# ASPARAGUS IN VARIATION

Servings: 2

*Remember to place pointed tips inward like spokes of a wheel so the tougher part of the stalks get the most heat.*

¾ lb. asparagus
2 tbs. water
2 tsp. olive oil

garnishes: shredded Romano cheese, toasted pine nuts, or pistachios

Snap off tough ends of asparagus and discard; peel stems. On a round microwaveable platter, arrange asparagus with tips toward center. Sprinkle with water, cover with vented plastic wrap and microwave on High for 2 to 3 minutes or just until tender, rotating platter once. Let stand 2 minutes; drain off juices. Drizzle asparagus with oil, turning to coat, and serve sprinkled with cheese, pine nuts or pistachios.

*per serving without garnishes*   77 calories, 5 g fat (1 g saturated fat), 0 mg cholesterol, 5 g protein, 6 g carbohydrate, 3 mg sodium

# ASPARAGUS OPEN SESAME

Servings: 2

*This Oriental dressing refreshes artichokes or green beans as well.*

¾ lb. asparagus spears, trimmed
and sliced on the diagonal
2 tbs. water
1 tbs. lemon juice
1 tbs. sesame oil

2 tsp. white wine vinegar
1 tbs. chopped cilantro
1 green onion (white part only),
chopped
dash pepper and fresh oregano

Place asparagus in a 1-quart casserole with water. Cover and microwave on High for about 4 minutes or until tender-crisp. Let stand 2 minutes. Combine lemon juice, sesame oil, vinegar, cilantro, onion, pepper and oregano; spoon over asparagus.

*per serving* 105 calories, 7 g fat (1 g saturated fat), 0 mg cholesterol, 5 g protein, 9 g carbohydrate, 5 mg sodium

# BAKED SPUDS WITH TOPPINGS

Servings: 1

*With a hearty topping, a baked potato becomes a fast easy dinner entrée.*

1 medium baking potato                your choice of topping

Prick potato with a fork in several places to allow steam to escape. Wrap in a paper towel and microwave on High for 3 minutes; turn potato over and microwave until tender, about 1½ to 2 minutes longer. Wrap in foil; let stand 5 minutes or until ready to serve. (Potato stays hot for 20 to 30 minutes.) Slit top of potato and squeeze open; add one of the toppings.

**Toppings**
- yogurt cheese or sour cream and finely chopped green onion or chives
- flaked smoky canned tuna, yogurt, and chopped Italian parsley
- diced smoked salmon, lowfat cream cheese, and fresh dill
- hot cooked mushrooms and lowfat herb cheese or chevre or Boursin
- chopped red and gold peppers and shredded Monterey Jack cheese
- feta, pitted Nicoise or ripe olives and diced cherry tomatoes

# BROCCOLI ITALIAN

Servings: 2

*Face the tender flower buds inward as they microwave — they cook faster than the fibrous stalks.*

¾ lb. broccoli florets
2 tbs. water
1 tsp. olive oil
1 tbs. pine nuts or pistachios

1 tsp. lemon zest
2 slices prosciutto or ham, cut in
  thin strips
2 lemon slices

Place broccoli and water in a casserole with flowers pointing inward and stalks outward. Cover with vented plastic wrap and microwave on High for 4 to 5 minutes or until crisp tender. Let stand 2 minutes; drain off any liquid. Place oil and nuts in a small baking dish, cover with a paper towel and microwave on High for 1 minute or until nuts are lightly toasted. Add lemon and prosciutto and microwave 30 seconds longer. Spoon over broccoli. Garnish with lemon slices.

*per serving*   187 calories, 12 g fat (2 g saturated fat), 16 mg cholesterol, 11 g protein, 13 g carbohydrate, 420 mg sodium

# ORANGE-GLAZED CARROTS AND PARSNIPS

Servings: 2

*The natural sweetness of parsnips complements carrots in this colorful side dish.*

2 medium carrots, peeled and sliced
2 medium parsnips, peeled and sliced
2 tbs. water
2 tbs. orange juice

1 tsp. olive oil or butter
1 tbs. honey
½ tsp. chopped ginger root
salt and pepper to taste

Place carrots and parsnips in a 1-quart casserole with the water. Cover tightly and microwave on High for 5 minutes or until tender-crisp. Drain. In a 1-cup measure, combine orange juice, oil, honey, and ginger root; microwave on High for 30 seconds or until heated through. Stir into vegetables. Season with salt and pepper.

---

*per serving*   261 calories, 3 g fat (.5 g saturated fat), 0 mg cholesterol, 4 g protein, 58 g carbohydrate, 49 mg sodium

---

# CORN IN THE HUSK

Servings: 2

*This is a neat, effortless way to cook corn, succulent and tender.*

2 ears corn                               butter, garlic butter or basil butter

Leave corn in husk. Run cold water over leaves and shake off well. Microwave on a platter, uncovered, for about 1½ to 2 minutes or until hot and cooked through. Serve with sweet butter or butter flavored with minced garlic or chopped basil.

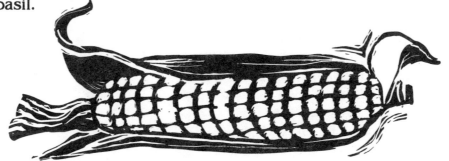

*per serving*   105 calories, 4 g fat (2 g saturated fat), 10 mg cholesterol, 2 g protein, 17 g carbohydrate, 42 mg sodium

# COUSCOUS WITH GREEN ONIONS

Servings: 2

*This is a fast cooking grain that makes an excellent accompaniment to fish or chicken.*

2 green onions
½ cup couscous
2 tsp. olive oil

¾ cup chicken stock
2 lemon slices

Make 2 green onion brushes with green ends of onions, cutting them in 1½-inch lengths. Chop remaining onions. In a 1-quart glass measure, place couscous, chopped onions, olive oil, and stock. Cover with vented plastic wrap and microwave on High for 3 to 4 minutes or until mixture boils and liquid is absorbed. Spoon into two 6-ounce custard cups or ramekins, patting down to make a compact timbale. Cover with plastic wrap and set aside until serving time. To serve, run a knife around edges of cups and invert onto dinner plates. Garnish with a lemon slice and an onion brush.

*per serving*   92 calories, 1 g fat (0 g saturated fat), 0 mg cholesterol, 3 g protein, 20 g carbohydrate, 562 mg sodium

# RATATOUILLE

*Eggplant, peppers and zucchini make a colorful melange in this classic Provençal dish.*

2 tbs. olive oil
1 clove garlic, minced
1 small onion, peeled and chopped
1 small slender Japanese eggplant, sliced
1 medium zucchini, sliced

1 small red pepper, seeded and thinly sliced
1 tbs. chopped fresh basil or ¼ tsp. dried
pepper to taste

In a 1½-quart casserole, combine oil, garlic, onion, eggplant, zucchini and pepper, turning to coat vegetables with oil. Cover tightly and microwave on High for 5 to 6 minutes or until vegetables are tender. Let stand 5 minutes. Sprinkle with basil and season with pepper to taste.

*per serving*   172 calories, 14 g fat (2 g saturated fat), 0 mg cholesterol, 2 g protein, 12 g carbohydrate, 7 mg sodium

# MARINATED RED AND GOLD PEPPERS

Servings: 2

*This makes a colorful accompaniment to pasta, fish or omelets.*

1 each red and gold pepper, halved,
  seeded and cut into ½-inch strips
2 tbs. chicken stock
1 tbs. olive oil
1 tbs. white wine vinegar
1 tbs. dry white wine
1 tsp. Dijon mustard

1 tsp. fresh oregano or ¼ tsp. dried
salt and pepper to taste
1 tomato, cut in wedges
¼ cup Nicoise-style or pitted ripe
  olives (optional)
Italian parsley or cilantro for garnish

Place peppers in a 9-inch pie plate and sprinkle with stock. Cover with vented plastic wrap and microwave on High for 2 to 3 minutes, stirring once. Let stand 2 minutes. In a bowl, stir together oil, vinegar, wine, mustard, oregano, salt and pepper. Drain peppers and toss with marinade. Cover and refrigerate until chilled. To serve, toss with tomatoes and olives. Garnish with parsley sprigs or chopped parsley.

*per serving*  102 calories, 7 g fat (1 g saturated fat), 0 mg cholesterol, 1 g protein, 8 g carbohydrate, 133 mg sodium

# ORIENTAL EGGPLANT

Servings: 2

*The slender Japanese eggplant of any hue — ivory, lavendar or purple — works well in this piquantly seasoned vegetable accompaniment or salad.*

1 small Japanese eggplant, halved
  vertically
peanut oil for rubbing
2 slices fresh ginger root, finely
  minced
1 clove garlic, minced

2 tsp. sesame oil
1 tbs. rice wine vinegar
½ tsp. honey or brown sugar
½ tsp. light soy sauce
1 green onion, chopped
minced cilantro for garnish

Rub cut surfaces of eggplant with peanut oil and wrap each half in waxed paper. Set on a pie plate and microwave on High for 4 to 5 minutes, turning halves once. Let stand 2 to 3 minutes. In a small bowl, combine ginger root, garlic, sesame oil, vinegar, honey and soy sauce. Cover with vented plastic wrap and microwave on High for about 20 seconds; stir to combine. Cut eggplant into chunks and toss in a serving bowl with sesame mixture. Sprinkle with green onions and cilantro. Serve warm or chilled.

*per serving*  78 calories, 5 g fat (1 g saturated fat), 0 mg cholesterol, 1 g protein, 9 g carbohydrate, 92 mg sodium

# SUGAR SNAPS AND PEAS

Servings: 2

*A handful of sugar snap peas from the garden or pea pods from the market uplifts the plebian pea.*

1 tsp. olive oil
1 green onion, chopped
1 cup shelled fresh peas or frozen
   petite peas, broken up

¼ lb. sugar snap peas or pea pods,
   strings removed

In a 1-quart casserole, combine oil and onions. Cook on High for 1 minute. Stir in peas. Cover tightly and cook on High 1½ to 2 minutes. Stir in snap peas. Cover and cook on High 1 minute longer or until tender-crisp.

Note: a shower of 1 tsp. chopped fresh tarragon makes a nice finish.

---

**per serving**   107 calories, 3 g fat (.5 g saturated fat), 0 mg cholesterol, 6 g protein, 16 g carbohydrate, 8 mg sodium

---

## Variation

Add 2 tbs. chopped prosciutto or ham to oil and green onion and cook as directed.

# PUMPKIN IN ORANGE SHELLS

Servings: 2

*The halloween jack-o-lantern or the deep orange garden pumpkin are excellent whipped and piled into saw-tooth orange shells. Winter squash such as butternut or Hubbard can also be used here. It is smart to cook a double batch of pumpkin or squash at one time, and then use it in a couple of styles.*

1 pound piece of pumpkin
1 orange

1 teaspoon brown sugar or honey
dash nutmeg

Place pumpkin in a shallow casserole cut-side up. Cover and microwave on High for 7 to 8 minutes or until tender when pierced with a fork, rotating dish once or twice. Let stand 5 minutes. Scoop out flesh and place 1½ cups in a bowl. Reserve remainder for another use. Cut orange in half zig-zag style and scoop out pulp; dice into segments. Mash pumpkin with half the segments, sugar and nutmeg. Pile into orange shells and top with remaining orange segments. Place on a shallow baking dish and microwave uncovered on High for 2 to 3 minutes or until hot through.

*per serving*   96 calories, 0 g fat (0 g saturated fat), 0 mg cholesterol, 2 g protein, 24 g carbohydrate, 3 mg sodium

# SHREDDED ZUCCHINI WITH HERBS

Servings: 2

*This is an excellent way to treat squash from the garden. Either green or gold zucchini work well.*

2 medium zucchini, shredded
salt
1 tbs. olive oil
1 clove garlic, minced
1 tsp. chopped fresh oregano or ¼ tsp. dried, or ⅛ tsp. freshly grated nutmeg
1 green onion, chopped
pepper to taste

In a bowl, sprinkle zucchini lightly with salt and let stand 15 minutes; rinse, drain and squeeze dry with paper towels. In a 1-quart casserole, place zucchini, oil, garlic, oregano and onion. Cover and microwave on High for 2 minutes or until crisp-tender. Season with pepper.

*per serving*   84 calories, 7 g fat (1 g saturated fat), 0 mg cholesterol, 2 g protein, 5 g carbohydrate, 6 mg sodium

# SLICED POTATOES AND TURNIPS WITH ROSEMARY

*Chicken broth bastes this overlapping interplay of potatoes and turnips which, when microwaved, become almost indistinguishable from each other in appearance.*

1 medium baking potato, peeled and thinly sliced
1 turnip, peeled and thinly sliced
1 tsp. fresh rosemary
½ clove garlic, minced
salt and pepper to taste
⅓ cup rich chicken stock

In a 9-inch pie plate, overlap alternating slices of potatoes and turnips. Scatter over rosemary and garlic; sprinkle with salt and pepper. Pour chicken stock over all. Cover with vented plastic wrap. Microwave on High for 5 minutes or until vegetables are barely tender. Let stand 5 minutes.

***per serving*** 309 calories, 1 g fat (0 g saturated fat), 0 mg cholesterol, 9 g protein, 69 g carbohydrate, 391 mg sodium

# RED SWISS CHARD SESAME

Servings: 1 or 2

*This zestful seasoning works well on spinach as well.*

2 cups chopped Swiss chard, ribs removed
1 tbs. balsamic vinegar
2 tsp. sesame oil
pepper to taste

Place Swiss chard in a 9-inch pie plate. Sprinkle with vinegar, oil and pepper. Cover with vented plastic wrap. Microwave on High for 3 minutes or until just tender. Makes 2 servings.

For 1 serving, divide ingredients and microwave on High for 1½ to 2 minutes.

***per serving*** 120 calories, 14 g fat (2 g saturated fat), 0 mg cholesterol, .5 g protein, 2 g carbohydrate, 77 mg sodium

# YOGURT GARLIC CHEESE

*This aromatic garlic sauce lends pizzaz to baked potatoes, still-warm broccoli, seafood or raw vegetables. Or spread over toasted French bread.*

6 cloves garlic, mashed
¼ cup chicken stock
1 tsp. fresh thyme or ¼ tsp. dried
2 tbs. *Yogurt Cheese*, page 17

In a small baking dish, place garlic, stock, and thyme. Cover with vented plastic wrap and microwave on High for about 3 minutes or until garlic is tender. Let stand 2 minutes. Place in a blender, add *Yogurt Cheese* and process until smooth. Serve at room temperature or chilled.

*per ¼ cup*   62 calories, 1 g fat (.5 g saturated fat), 2 mg cholesterol, 4 g protein, 9 g carbohydrate, 224 mg sodium

# MEAT ENTRÉES

# FETTUCINE WITH HAM AND PEAS

*A mixed green salad and crusty French bread are pleasing accompaniments to this fast pasta entrée. If sugar snap peas or snow peas are available, add a handful to the creamy sauce.*

6 oz. fettucine, cooked according
  to package instructions
2 tbs. olive oil
2 cloves garlic, minced
½ cup fresh green peas or frozen
  petite peas, thawed

¼ cup minced ham or prosciutto
¼ cup heavy cream
⅓ cup grated Parmesan or Romano
  cheese
freshly ground pepper to taste

While pasta cooks, place oil, garlic, peas and ham or prosciutto in a 2-quart casserole. Cover and cook on High 2 minutes or until hot through. Add cream and cheese; microwave on Medium for 1 minute or until cheese is melted. Drain pasta, add to sauce and toss lightly to coat. Season with pepper. Serve at once.

***per serving*** 478 calories, 31 g fat (12 g saturated fat), 63 mg cholesterol, 18 g protein, 32 g carbohydrate, 556 mg sodium

# GRILLED BEEF AND SUMMER VEGETABLES

Servings: 2

*This makes a savory summer salad entrée plate. If desired, grill a flank steak one night and have it hot. Then use the balance in this salad combination the next night. The meat may also be broiled.*

*Red Wine Marinade*, follows
½ lb. flank steak
1 Japanese eggplant, sliced diagonally
1 red pepper, halved, seeded and cut in strips
1 small red onion, peeled and cut in wedges
4 mushrooms
1 tbs. olive oil
1 tsp. balsamic vinegar
1 clove garlic, minced
1 tsp. fresh rosemary or ¼ tsp. dried
1½ cups choice mixed salad greens
2 sprigs rosemary

Combine *Red Wine Marinade* and let meat marinate for at least 1 to 2 hours. Place on a grill or broiling pan; alongside place vegetables. Mix together oil, vinegar, garlic and rosemary; brush over vegetables and meat. Broil or grill over hot coals for 8 to 10 minutes or until cooked medium rare. Let meat cool slightly and slice thinly. Place meat on plates with vegetables alongside. Garnish with rosemary sprigs.

### Red Wine Marinade

¼ cup dry red wine
2 tsp. olive oil
1 tsp. fresh rosemary sprigs or ¼ tsp. dried
1 clove garlic, minced

Combine ingredients in a bowl.

---

***per serving***   476 calories, 23 g fat (5 g saturated fat), 101 mg cholesterol, 39 g protein, 32 g carbohydrate, 99 mg sodium

---

# ROLLED HAM AND SPUD PLATTER DINNER

Servings: 1 or 2

*This color-laden plate makes an appealing presentation and offers lots of healthy dining.*

3 small red-skinned new potatoes, sliced, unpeeled
1 small golden or green zucchini squash, sliced in a fan
½ cup shredded spinach
1 green onion, chopped
1 tsp. fresh thyme or rosemary or ¼ tsp. dried

salt and pepper to taste
¼ cup chicken stock
3 to 4 oz. thinly sliced boiled or Black Forest ham, rolled
3 or 4 red cherry tomatoes
Dijon mustard

On a microwaveable dinner plate, arrange overlapping slices of potato in a semi-circle on one outer side of the plate. Arrange squash on the opposite side, separating slices slightly like a fan. Place spinach in the center and sprinkle with onion, thyme, salt and pepper. Pour chicken stock over all and cover with vented plastic wrap. Microwave on High for 5 minutes. Place ham rolls on spinach. Cover with plastic wrap and microwave on High 1 to 1½ minutes or until hot through. Let stand 5 minutes. Garnish with cherry tomatoes and accompany with Dijon mustard. Makes 1 serving.

For 2 servings, double the recipe and arrange 2 plates. Microwave them separately as per directions.

*per serving*  520 calories, 8 g fat (2.5 g saturated fat), 59 mg cholesterol, 36 g protein, 80 g carbohydrate, 2156 mg sodium

# FRENCHMAN'S BURGERS

*A shallot-laced wine sauce gilds these fast burgers.*

8 to 10 oz. lean ground chuck
salt and pepper to taste
2 tsp. Dijon mustard
1 clove garlic, minced
¼ tsp. dried thyme
1 tsp. olive oil

1 shallot, chopped
1 clove garlic, minced
¼ cup each beef stock and dry red
  wine
2 tsp. butter
1 tbs. minced parsley

Mix together ground chuck, salt, pepper, mustard, garlic and thyme. Shape into 2 patties. Heat a large frying pan over medium high heat, add oil, and sauté meat patties until browned on both sides, about 3 minutes on a side for rare meat. Transfer to hot plates. Add shallot and second garlic clove to drippings; cook just until glazed. Pour in stock and wine; cook down until reduced by half. Remove from heat; swirl in butter and parsley. Spoon sauce over hamburgers.

***per serving***   548 calories, 39 g fat (16 g saturated fat), 137 mg cholesterol, 36 g protein, 7 g carbohydrate, 356 mg sodium

# LAMB SKEWERS MOROCCAN

Servings: 2

*Either lamb or turkey works well in this spicy skewer.*

### Yogurt Marinade

1½ tsp. curry powder
⅛ tsp. *each* ground cinnamon and
    allspice

1 tbs. lemon juice
¼ cup unflavored lowfat yogurt
2 tsp. sesame oil

8 oz. boneless lamb leg or turkey
    breast, cut into 1-inch cubes
4 pearl onions, peeled and parboiled

4 mushrooms
arugula or cilantro

In a bowl stir together curry powder, cinnamon, allspice, lemon juice, yogurt and sesame oil. Add lamb cubes and let marinate 1 hour or longer. Thread meat cubes on skewers, starting and ending with an onion and alternating the mushrooms between. Grill or broil about 8 to 10 minutes or until cooked through, basting once or twice with remaining marinade. Serve on a bed or arugula or cilantro.

*per serving* 378 calories, 24 g fat (10 g saturated fat), 112 mg cholesterol, 30 g protein, 9 g carbohydrate, 100 mg sodium

# HUNTER'S STYLE SAUSAGE PLATTER DINNER

Servings: 1 or 2

*Italian flavors star in this eye-catching plate that struts the colors of the Italian flag. If the specialty sausage is unavailable, substitute a poached or cooked regular Italian-style sausage.*

1 small, slender Japanese eggplant, sliced
1 small zucchini, sliced diagonally
½ cup red pepper strips
4 red onion rings
2 tsp. fresh basil, chopped, or ½ tsp. dried
salt and pepper to taste
¼ cup chicken stock
1 cooked whiskey fennel or Italian-style sausage, about 4 oz.

On a microwaveable dinner plate, arrange overlapping slices of eggplant n a semi-circle on one outer side of the plate. Arrange zucchini slices on the opposite outer side. Place pepper strips and onion rings in the center, sprinkle with basil, salt and pepper, and pour chicken stock over all. Cover with vented plastic wrap and microwave on High for 5 minutes. Place sausage on peppers and onions, cover with plastic wrap, and microwave on High 1 to 1½ minutes or until hot through. Let stand 5 minutes. Makes 1 serving.

For 2 servings, double the recipe and arrange 2 plates. Microwave them separately as per directions.

*per serving*   513 calories, 36 g fat (12.5 g saturated fat), 94 mg cholesterc , 27 g protein, 22 g carbohydrate, 1848 mg sodium

# SUGAR SNAPS AND SAUSAGE PLATTER DINNER

Servings: 1 or 2

*This makes a colorful plate of gold, green, scarlet and white vegetables and fruit as a backdrop to the plump peppery sausage. Cut the squash in 4 or 5 lengthwise slashes, leaving the stem end uncut for about ¾ inch. This way the squash can fan out in cooking.*

3 small red-skinned new potatoes, sliced, unpeeled
1 small golden or green zucchini squash, sliced in a fan
8 sugar snap peas
1 green onion, chopped
1 tsp. fresh thyme or rosemary or ¼ tsp. dried
salt and pepper to taste
¼ cup chicken stock
1 cooked Kielbasa or chicken-apple sausage or duck and beef with
   green peppercorns sausage (about 4 to 5 oz.)
½ red-skinned Bartlett or Comice pear

On a microwaveable dinner plate, arrange overlapping slices of potato in a semi-circle on one outer side of the plate. Arrange squash on the opposite side, separating slices slightly like a fan. Place sugar snap peas in the center and sprinkle with onion, thyme and salt and pepper. Pour over chicken stock and cover with vented plastic wrap. Microwave on High for 5 minutes. Place sausage on the peas and flank with pear slices. Cover with plastic wrap and microwave on High 1 to 1½ minutes or until hot through. Let stand 5 minutes. Makes 1 serving.

For 2 servings, double the recipe and arrange 2 plates. Microwave them separately as per directions.

**per serving** 742 calories, 32 g fat (12 g saturated fat), 76 mg cholesterol, 26 g protein, 91 g carbohydrate, 1620 mg sodium

# PICADILLO

*This spicy meat sauce is fun to tuck into a tortilla for an easy taco or spoon inside split baked potatoes. Serve it also as a topping for Italian green beans.*

½ tsp. olive oil
1 clove garlic, minced
½ cup chopped onion
½ lb. ground pork or turkey
1 tomato, peeled, seeded and chopped
1 tsp. chili powder
1 tbs. red wine vinegar

½ tsp. brown sugar
¼ tsp. ground cinnamon
¼ tsp. ground allspice
salt and pepper to taste
3 tbs. raisins
½ cup shredded Monterey Jack or
  Muenster cheese

In a 1-quart casserole, combine oil, garlic and onion. Cook on High for 1 to 2 minutes, or until onion is soft. Stir in ground meat, spreading it evenly over dish. Cook on High for 3 to 4 minutes or until just a slight pink color remains, stirring once. Drain. Add tomatoes, chili powder, vinegar, sugar, cinnamon, allspice, salt, pepper and raisins. Cook on High for 4 to 5 minutes or until most moisture has cooked away. Sprinkle with cheese and cook on Medium for 30 seconds to 1 minute or until cheese is melted.

***per serving*** 583 calories, 38 g fat (17 g saturated fat), 143 mg cholesterol, 40 g protein, 19 g carbohydrate, 315 mg sodium

# PORK SATES

*Hot grilled nectarine halves and mushrooms enhance these zestful pork kebobs.*

½ tsp. grated ginger root
3 tbs. chutney
1 tbs. *each* olive oil, catsup and chili
  sauce
1 tsp. each honey and soy sauce
1 clove garlic, minced

dash liquid hot pepper seasoning
8 oz. boneless pork loin, cut into
  1-inch pieces
6 mushroom caps
1 nectarine, halved and pitted
mint or cilantro for garnish

In a blender, place ginger, chutney, oil, catsup, chili sauce, honey, soy sauce, garlic and pepper seasoning; blend until smooth. Pour into a bowl. Add meat and let marinate 1 hour or longer, turning occasionally. Impale meat on skewers and broil 10 to 12 minutes, turning to brown all sides. Brush mushrooms and nectarines with remaining marinade and add to skewers the last 3 to 4 minutes to heat through and glaze. Serve on a plate garnished with mint.

---

***per serving*** 531 calories, 39 g fat (12 g saturated fat), 116 mg cholesterol, 32 g protein, 13 g carbohydrate, 246 mg sodium

# PITA PIZZA ITALIAN-STYLE

Servings: 1 or 2

*Whole wheat pita breads made a flavor-packed base for a quick pizza.*

3 tbs. pizza sauce, flavored tomato sauce or tomato paste
1 whole wheat pita bread (6-inch diameter), split horizontally into 2 pieces
⅔ cup thinly sliced zucchini
3 tbs. chopped red or sweet onion
½ cup chopped tomato or halved cherry tomatoes
2 to 3 tbs. pitted ripe or Nicoise-style olives
2 oz. boiled ham, prosciutto or salami, slivered
2 tsp. chopped fresh basil or ½ tsp. dried
¼ cup shredded mozzarella or Fontina cheese

Spread pizza sauce on pita halves and lay on paper towels on small microwaveable plates. Place zucchini and onion in a 2-cup casserole. Microwave uncovered on High until crisp tender, about 1½ to 2 minutes. Stir in tomato, olives, ham or prosciutto and basil. Spoon onto pita halves; top with cheese.

Microwave uncovered on High until hot, about 1 to 2 minutes. Cut into wedges. Makes 2 servings.

For 1 serving, divide ingredients in half. Microwave zucchini and onion about 1 minute. Microwave pizza on High about 45 to 60 seconds.

*per serving*  644 calories, 17 g fat (8 g saturated fat), 52 mg cholesterol, 17 g protein, 28 g carbohydrate, 1001 mg sodium

# BEEF BIRDS SPIEDINI

*Either beef or veal works well for this fast Italian-style entrée that is excellent hot or cold for summer fare.*

8 oz. sirloin tip beef roast, sliced very thin or veal cutlets, cut very thin
salt and pepper to taste
2 tsp. fresh chopped oregano or thyme or ¼ tsp. dried
2 oz. Fontina cheese, thinly sliced
2 oz. boiled ham or prosciutto
2 tsp. olive oil
1 tsp. balsamic vinegar
½ clove garlic, minced

Pound meat between 2 sheets of waxed paper until very thin, making rectangles about 3 by 5 inches. Sprinkle with salt, pepper and oregano. Lay a slice of cheese and one of prosciutto on each slice of meat. Roll up from narrow end. Thread 2 or 3 meat rolls on a skewer. Combine oil, vinegar and garlic; brush over meat. Broil or grill over medium-hot coals, turning to brown all sides.

*per serving*  593 calories, 45 g fat (17 g saturated fat), 150 mg cholesterol, 45 g protein, 1 g carbohydrate, 727 mg sodium

# FISH AND SHELLFISH ENTRÉES

# CRAB TORTILLA PIZZA

Servings: 1 or 2

*A flour tortilla forms an instant pizza base for this hot seafood sandwich.*

2 tbs. tomato paste
1/4 tsp. dried tarragon
1 shallot or green onion, chopped
1 8-inch flour tortilla
2 oz. crab meat or small cooked shrimp

2 to 3 sun-dried tomatoes, snipped
2 mushrooms, sliced
2 tbs. shredded Monterey Jack or
  Jarlsberg cheese
1 tbs. chopped Italian parsley

Place tomato paste, tarragon and shallot in a custard cup and microwave on High 30 seconds to 1 minute, to soften shallot. Place tortilla on 2 sheets of paper towel on a microwaveable plate. Spread with tomato paste mixture. Scatter over crab, tomatoes, mushrooms, and cheese. Microwave on High 2 to 3 minutes, rotating once, until cheese melts. Sprinkle with parsley and serve.

For 2 servings, double ingredients and microwave each pizza separately.

For conventional cooking, place pizza in a baking dish and bake in a 400° oven for 6 to 8 minutes.

*per serving*  501 calories, 22 g fat (12 g saturated fat), 88 mg cholesterol, 33 g protein, 49 g carbohydrate, 649 mg sodium

# LINGUINE WITH CLAM SAUCE

Servings: 2

*This is a handy dish to make with ingredients generally in the pantry. Star anise gives the pasta an intriguing flavor.*

6 oz. linguine
1 star anise or ¼ tsp. anise seeds
2 tbs. olive oil
1 clove garlic, minced
1 green onion, chopped
1 tsp. fresh chopped oregano

1 can (5 oz.) whole clams
¼ cup dry white wine
1 small tomato, chopped
1 tbs. chopped parsley
¼ cup shredded Parmesan or
  Romano cheese

Cook linguine and star anise conventionally in boiling salted water, following package instructions. In a 1-quart casserole combine oil, garlic, and onion and microwave, uncovered, on High for 1 minute. Add oregano, clams, wine, and tomato, cover with vented plastic wrap, and microwave on High for 3 to 4 minutes or until hot through. Drain pasta. Spoon onto plates and top with clam sauce. Sprinkle with parsley and cheese.

*per serving*   441 calories, 20 g fat (4 g saturated fat), 57 mg cholesterol, 28 g protein, 33 g carbohydrate, 323 mg sodium

# ZITI WITH SMOKED SALMON

Servings: 2

*Use any tubular pasta in this elegant entrée featuring smoked salmon in a dill cream sauce.*

6 ounces ziti or any tubular pasta
1 tbs. olive oil
1 clove garlic, minced
1 shallot, chopped
2 tomatoes, cored, peeled and cut into - inch cubes
1/3 cup heavy cream
2 tbs. Pernod or pepper vodka

freshly ground pepper to taste
1/4 lb. sliced smoked salmon, cut into 1 1/2 inch st ips
2 tsp. chopped fresh dill or 1/2 tsp. dried
3 tbs. chopped Italian parsley
1/3 cup freshly grated Parmesan

Cook ziti in boiling salted water according to package directions; drain. In a 2-quart casserole, place oil, garlic and shallot, turning to coat. Cover with vented plastic wrap and cook on High 45 seconds. Add tomatoes, cream, Pernod or pepper vodka and microwave uncovered for 2 minutes, or until bubbly. Add salmon, dill and parsley. Microwave 30 seconds to heat through. Add drained pasta and cheese; toss to coat.

**per serving**   538 calories, 30 g fat (14 g saturated fat), 81 mg cholesterol, 24 g protein, 37 g carbohydrate, 787 mg sodium

# FISH FILLETS MEXICALI

*Golden peppers and green onions make a festive accent on this spicy tomato sauce that blankets snowy fish fillets.*

2 green onions, chopped
½ cup slivered gold bell pepper strips
1 large tomato, peeled and chopped
1 clove garlic, minced
⅛ tsp. cumin
1 tsp. fresh oregano or ¼ tsp. dried
1 tsp. chopped ginger root

½ lb. turbot or sole fillets
salt and pepper to taste
1 tbs. each chopped Italian parsley
  and cilantro
½ avocado
lime or lemon wedges for garnish

In a 9-inch pie plate, place onions, pepper and tomato; microwave on High 1½ to 2 minutes to soften. Add garlic, cumin, oregano and ginger root; microwave 30 seconds. Slip fish fillets under sauce and sprinkle with salt, pepper, parsley and cilantro. Cover with vented plastic wrap and microwave on High for 1½ to 2 minutes or until fish turns opaque. Let stand 2 to 3 minutes. Serve on plates. Garnish with avocado slices and lime wedges.

*per serving*   136 calories, 2 g fat (.5 g saturated fat), 54 mg cholesterol, 23 g protein, 7 g carbohydrate, 104 mg sodium

# FISH SURPRISE IN A BAG

Servings: 1 or 2

*Small white paper bags make neat containers for cooking fish steaks and shredded greens. Parchment paper can also be cut and folded, replacing the bags.*

2 small white paper bags
⅓ cup finely shredded or chopped radicchio or spinach leaves
⅓ cup finely shredded or chopped Belgian endive or curly endive leaves
2 green onions, finely chopped
2 or 3 mushrooms, thinly sliced
8 oz. fish fillets or steaks: shark, halibut, mahi mahi, or salmon, cut into 2
   equal pieces or 1-inch cubes
salt and pepper to taste
1 tsp. chopped tarragon or ¼ tsp. dried
2 lemon slices
2 tbs. dry white wine

Cut off the top 4 inches of the bags to make them easier to work with. Place on a baking dish and into them divide radicchio, endive leaves, onions and mushrooms. Arrange fish on top and season with salt, pepper and tarragon. Cover with lemon slices and drizzle with wine. Fold down bag tops, slash 2 holes in each with a wire skewer and then slip a wooden toothpick into the holes to secure the fold in place. Microwave on High for 2 minutes or until fish turns opaque. Let stand 2 minutes. Makes 2 servings.

For 1 serving, halve the ingredients, prepare 1 bag and microwave on High for 1 minute.

For conventional cooking, place bags of fish on a baking dish and bake in a preheated 425° oven for 8 to 10 minutes or until cooked through.

**per serving**   152 calories, 3 g fat (.5 g saturated fat), 36 mg cholesterol, 25 g protein, 5 g carbohydrate, 139 mg sodium

# LEMON HALIBUT AND
# SPINACH PLATTER DINNER

Servings: 1 or 2

*This succulent fish plate interweaves spinach, mushrooms, cucumbers and new potatoes with shark in a shower of lemon zest and parsley.*

4 oz. halibut or shark, cut into 1-inch chunks
1 tbs. lemon juice
1 tsp. chopped ginger root
2 tsp. lemon zest
2 tbs. chopped parsley
3 red-skinned new potatoes, sliced
6 slices cucumber or 1 summer squash, sliced
3/4 cup finely cut spinach leaves
6 button mushrooms, sliced
salt and pepper to taste
1/4 cup chicken stock

In a small bowl, toss fish with lemon juice and ginger root; add half the lemon zest and parsley; let stand a few minutes. On a microwaveable dinner plate, arrange overlapping slices of potato in a semi-circle on one outer side of plate. Arrange cucumber slices on opposite outer side. Place spinach and mushrooms in center; sprinkle with remaining lemon zest, parsley, salt and pepper. Pour chicken stock over all and cover with vented plastic wrap. Microwave on High for 5 minutes. Place fish on spinach and mushrooms. Cover with plastic wrap and microwave on High 1 to 1½ minutes or until fish is barely cooked through. Let stand 5 minutes. Makes 1 serving.

For 2 servings, double the recipe and arrange 2 plates. Microwave them separately as per directions.

*per serving*   493 calories, 4 g fat (.5 g saturated fat), 36 mg cholesterol, 34 g protein, 84 g carbohydrate, 496  mg sodium

# CRAB AND JICAMA SHELLS

Servings: 1 or 2

*Jicama lends a sweet crunchiness to these fast seafood ramekins that are attractive baked in scallop shells.*

8 oz. crab meat or small cooked
  shrimp
3/4 cup jicama, cut into matchstick
  pieces
2 green onions, chopped

2 tbs. dry white wine
2 tbs. *Mustard Vinaigrette,* page 30
2 tsp. fresh chopped tarragon or 1/2
  tsp. dried
2 tsp. pine nuts or pistachios

In a bowl lightly mix together crab, jicama, onions, wine, *Mustard Vinaigrette* and tarragon. Spoon into 2 scallop shells or other ramekins. Sprinkle with nuts. Cover with vented plastic wrap. Microwave on High for 1½ to 2 minutes or until heated through. Makes 2 servings.

For 1 serving, halve the ingredients and microwave on High for about 1 minute.

---

***per serving***   183 calories, 4 g fat (.5 g saturated fat), 75 mg cholesterol, 24 g protein, 10 g carbohydrate, 353 mg sodium

---

# MUSSELS IN A WINE BATH

Servings: 1 or 2

*Mussels are a treat served in soup bowls with herb-laced wine juices. Littleneck clams also work well. Serve with sourdough bread or sweet French bread.*

1¼ lbs. mussels or littleneck clams
1 tbs. olive oil
3 tbs. dry white wine
2 green onions, chopped

1 clove garlic, minced
1 tbs. chopped Italian parsley
1 tbs. chopped fresh dill

Scrub seafood well under cold running water; remove any beards from mussels. Arrange around outside edge of a 9-inch pie plate. Combine olive oil, wine, onions and garlic. Spoon over mussels. Cover with vented plastic wrap; microwave on High for 2½ to 5 minutes or until mussels open, rotating dish once. Discard any that do not open. Let stand for 2 minutes. Serve seafood in 2 bowls with juices. Sprinkle with parsley and dill. Accompany with bread. Makes 2 entrée servings.

For 1 serving, halve ingredients and microwave on High 1½ to 4 minutes.

For conventional cooking, cook mussels with juices in a saucepot, simmering just until shells open, about 6 to 8 minutes.

**per serving**  334 calories, 14 g fat (2 g saturated fat), 80 mg cholesterol, 35 g protein, 14 g carbohydrate, 820 mg sodium

# ORIENTAL TROUT

Servings: 2

*This is an excellent marinade for any cleaned whole fish or fish steaks.*

1 whole salmon trout or lake trout,
  head removed (about 14 oz.)
1 tbs. soy sauce
2 tsp. dry sherry

1½ tsp. hoisin sauce
1 tsp. sesame oil
1 tsp. finely chopped ginger root
1 green onion, julienned

Diagonally slash fish skin 3 times on each side. Place on a microwaveable dish. Combine soy sauce, sherry, hoisin sauce, sesame oil and ginger root; spoon into fish cavity and over fish. Let marinate for at least 15 minutes or longer. Sprinkle fish with onion; cover with vented plastic wrap. Microwave on High for 3 to 4 minutes or until fish is opaque and flakes with a fork close to the backbone, rotating dish once or twice and basting with marinade halfway through. Makes 2 servings.

For conventional cooking, place fish in a baking dish and bake in a preheated 425° oven for about 8 to 10 minutes or until just cooked through.

*per serving*  334 calories, 11 g fat (2 g saturated fat), 145 mg cholesterol, 53 g protein, 2 g carbohydrate, 242 mg sodium

# SALMON IN GRAPE LEAVES

Servings: 1 or 2

*Bottled grape leaves make a tangy wrapper on salmon fillets for a festive entrée.*

4 bottled grape leaves
8 oz. salmon fillets
4 tsp. lemon zest
1 green onion, chopped
salt and pepper to taste

2 tbs. golden raisins
¼ cup white wine
2 tsp. olive oil
2 tbs. toasted pine nuts or pistachios

On a work surface, overlap 2 grape leaves slightly, divide salmon in half and place half on each of the grape leaves. Repeat with remaining grape leaves and salmon. Sprinkle with 2 tsp. of the lemon zest, onion, salt and pepper. Fold in sides of grape leaves and roll up for both packets. Place on a 9-inch pie plate. Sprinkle with remaining lemon zest and raisins, and drizzle with wine and olive oil. Cover with waxed paper. Microwave on high for 2 to 3 minutes or until fish flakes with a fork, rotating dish once or twice. Scatter nuts on top of each packet. Makes 2 servings.

For 1 serving, prepare half the recipe and microwave on High 1 to 1½ minutes.

*per serving*  386 calories, 25 g fat (3.5 g saturated fat), 63 mg cholesterol, 24 g protein, 12 g carbohydrate, 118 mg sodium

# ROMAINE-WRAPPED FISH BUNDLES

Servings: 1 or 2

*Romaine leaves wrap up these neat fish packets for an eye-catching entrée that's swift and succulent. Swiss chard leaves also work well.*

8 large romaine lettuce leaves
8 oz. shark, orange roughy, halibut or other white fish without bones
2 green onions, chopped
2 tsp. orange zest
2 tbs. minced Italian parsley
salt and pepper to taste
¼ cup dry white wine
4 orange slices

Rinse leaves in cold water; shake off excess. Place on a 9-inch pie plate and microwave on High for 20 seconds or until limp. On a work surface, overlap 2 lettuce leaves slightly. Top with half the fish, cut into 1- inch cubes, if desired. Mix onions, orange zest and parsley; sprinkle ½ of it over fish. Season with salt and pepper. Fold lettuce carefully around fish, tucking in ends to form a package. Transfer to a pie plate, seam side down. Repeat with second fish bundle.

Pour wine over bundles. Cover with vented plastic wrap. Microwave on High for 2 minutes; rotate plate and microwave for 30 seconds longer or until fish is opaque. Garnish with orange slices. Makes 2 servings.

For 1 serving, halve ingredients and microwave about 1½ minutes.

___

**per serving**   179 calories, 3 g fat (0 g saturated fat), 36 mg cholesterol, 25 g protein, 8 g carbohydrate, 73 mg sodium

___

## Variation

Pickled ginger slices add a sprightly zip when 2 or 3 are rolled up in each fish bundle.

# SCALLOPS ALMONDINE

Servings: 1 or 2

*The tiny bay scallops cook faster than the larger sea scallops, so watch timing carefully.*

2 tbs. sliced almonds
1 tsp. olive oil
2 tbs. vermouth or very dry white wine
1 tsp. chopped tarragon or ¼ tsp. dried

½ lb. scallops
salt and pepper to taste
watercress sprigs or chopped Italian
 parsley for garnish

Place nuts in a shallow baking dish and microwave on High for 1 to 2 minutes or until lightly toasted. In a 9-inch pie plate, place oil, wine, and tarragon. Swish scallops in mixture and arrange in a ring around outside of dish. Season with salt and pepper. Cover with waxed paper and microwave on Medium for 2 to 3 minutes or until just opaque and resilient to the touch. Let stand 2 minutes. To serve, sprinkle with almonds and garnish with watercress or parsley. Makes 2 servings.

For 1 serving, divide ingredients in half and microwave 1 to 2 minutes or until scallops are opaque.

*per serving*   161 calories, 6 g fat (1 g saturated fat), 37 mg cholesterol, 20 g protein, 4 g carbohydrate,184 mg sodium

# SCAMPI WITH HERBS

*Butterflied shrimp marinate in a wine bath and then fast-cook for a succulent entrée.*

1 tbs. each dry vermouth and lemon juice
1½ tsp. olive oil
1 clove garlic, minced
1 tbs. chopped Italian parsley
1 green onion, chopped

1 tsp. fresh oregano or ¼ tsp. dried
salt and pepper to taste
½ lb. large fresh shrimp
chopped Italian parsley for garnish
lemon wedges for garnish

In a 9-inch pie plate mix together vermouth, lemon juice, oil, garlic, parsley, onion, oregano, salt and pepper. Shell shrimp bodies, leaving tail shells intact, and split shrimp meat half way to tail, washing out sand vein. Let marinate in the dressing for 30 minutes. Arrange shrimp in a circle around outer edge of dish, tails inward. Cover with vented plastic wrap and microwave on High until shrimp turn pink, about 1½ to 2 minutes. Let stand for 2 minutes. Sprinkle with chopped parsley and garnish with lemon wedges.

*per serving* 156 calories, 5 g fat (1 g saturated fat), 221 mg cholesterol, 24 g protein, 2 g carbohydrate, 256 mg sodium

# SHRIMP WINTER PLATTER DINNER

Servings: 1 or 2

*This colorful plate can vary with vegetables of the season.*

1 parsnip or carrot, peeled and sliced
½ cup red or gold pepper strips
½ cup sugar snap peas, strings removed
1 green onion, chopped
1 tsp. fresh tarragon or dill or ¼ tsp. dried

salt and pepper to taste
¼ cup chicken stock
½ pound medium or small cooked shrimp
2 tsp. sweet hot mustard
1 tsp. lemon juice

On a microwaveable dinner plate, arrange overlapping slices of parsnip in a semi-circle on one outer side of plate. Arrange pepper strips on opposite outer side. Place sugar snaps in center and sprinkle with green onions. Season with tarragon or dill, salt and pepper. Pour chicken stock over and cover with vented plastic wrap. Microwave on High for 5 minutes. Place shrimp on sugar snap peas; mix mustard and lemon juice together and spread over shrimp. Cover with plastic wrap and microwave on High 1 minute or until hot through. Let stand 5 minutes. Makes 1 serving.

For 2 servings, double recipe, arrange 2 plates and microwave separately.

Optional winter vegetables: sliced fennel, sliced button mushrooms or halved Brussels sprouts.

## Summer Variation

For vegetables substitute sliced yellow or green zucchini, sliced Japanese eggplant, snow pea pods, and include red or yellow peppers.

*per serving*   401 calories, 5 g fat (1 g saturated fat), 442 mg cholesterol, 54 g protein, 36 g carbohydrate, 1291mg sodium

# SHRIMP WITH FETA

Servings: 2

*This was a discovery in the Greek islands where waterfront tavernas serve this dish in piping hot clay ramekins.*

1 tbs. lemon juice
½ lb. raw medium shrimp, shelled
  and deveined
2 tsp. olive oil
⅓ cup chopped onions
1 clove garlic, minced
½ cup tomato puree
3 tbs. dry white wine and clam juice

1 tbs. Pernod or anise-flavored
  liqueur or brandy
1 tsp. fresh chopped oregano or ¼
  tsp. dried
1 tbs. chopped parsley
2 oz. feta cheese, cut into ½-inch
  cubes

Pour lemon juice over shrimp and let stand a few minutes. In a 2-quart baking dish, place oil and onions; cover with waxed paper and microwave on High for 1 minute. Add garlic, tomato puree, wine and clam juice. Microwave on High for 2 to 3 minutes or until boiling. Add shrimp, cover with vented plastic wrap and microwave on High just until they turn pink, about 1½ minutes. Remove from microwave. In a small ovenproof bowl, warm Pernod for 10 seconds in microwave, ignite, and pour over shrimp. Sprinkle with oregano and parsley; scatter feta over top. Serve in individual ramekins.

For conventional cooking, bake shrimp in a 400° oven for 10 to 15 minutes or until hot through. Then flame with Pernod and garnish with herbs and feta.

*per serving*  299 calories, 13 g fat (5 g saturated fat), 198 mg cholesterol, 29 g protein, 12 g carbohydrate, 499 mg sodium

# SNAPPER WITH PEPPERS AND PEARS

Servings: 2

*Brilliant red peppers and pears stripe white fish fillets with a bit of drama.*

*Cilantro Dressing*, page 101
2 snapper fillets, 8 to 10 oz. each
1 Bartlett or Anjou pear, halved,
  seeded and sliced
½ red pepper, halved, seeded and
  cut into lengthwise strips

1 green onion, chopped
dash hot pepper sauce
cilantro or mint for garnish

Prepare *Cilantro Dressing*. Place fish fillets on a broiling pan, brush with dressing and broil 2 minutes. Top each fillet with pear and pepper slices, alternating three pear slices and 2 pepper slices in a row on each fillet. Brush with dressing. Continue broiling 2 minutes longer or until fish barely flakes when pressed. Place fish on plates and scatter with onions. Garnish with a few sprigs of cilantro or mint.

## Cilantro Dressing

1 tsp. julienned orange peel
1 tbs. lemon juice
2 tbs. orange juice
2 tsp. olive oil

1 green onion, chopped
dash hot pepper sauce
1 tbs. chopped cilantro or mint

Stir ingredients together.

*per serving* 483 calories, 18 g fat (3 g saturated fat), 105 mg cholesterol, 60 g protein, 21 g carbohydrate, 192 mg sodium

# FILLET OF SOLE FLORENTINE

Servings: 2

*A bed of spinach makes a flavor-packed backdrop for fish. A few cooked chanterelles or shiitake mushrooms make an excellent addition to the spinach.*

2 green onions, chopped
2 cups chopped spinach
2 tsp. olive oil
3 tbs. dry white wine
2 sole fillets (about 8 oz.)
salt and pepper to taste

1 tsp. fresh tarragon or ¼ tsp. dried
3 tbs. sour cream
2 tbs. shredded Parmesan or Romano
 cheese
paprika

In a 9-inch pie plate, place onions and spinach, making a bed of greens. Combine oil and wine; drizzle half of it over spinach. Cover with vented plastic wrap and microwave on High for 1½ minutes or until barely soft. Top with fish, season with salt and pepper, and sprinkle with tarragon. Pour remaining wine mixture over all. Cover with vented plastic wrap and microwave on High 1½ minutes or until fish starts to turn opaque. Spread fish with sour cream, sprinkle with cheese and dust with paprika. Microwave on High 30 seconds.

*per serving*   254 calories, 13 g fat (5 g saturated fat), 69 mg cholesterol, 27 g protein, 5 g carbohydrate, 269 mg sodium

# SOLE VERONIQUE

Servings: 1 or 2

*Juicy hot grapes spark this almost instant fish bake.*

8 oz. sole or turbot fillets
2 tbs. dry white wine
1 tsp. lemon juice
2 tsp. julienned lemon peel

pepper to taste
½ cup green or red seedless grapes
watercress sprigs for garnish

Place fish fillets in a 9-inch pie plate. In a small bowl, stir together wine, lemon juice, lemon peel, pepper and grapes. Spoon over fish. Cover with waxed paper. Microwave on High for 2 minutes or until fish turns opaque. Let stand 2 to 3 minutes. Serve garnished with watercress. Makes 2 servings.

For 1 serving, divide ingredients in half and microwave on High for 1 minute or until fish turns opaque.

For conventional cooking, bake sole with grapes in a baking dish in a preheated 425° oven for 8 to 10 minutes or until cooked through.

*per serving*   143 calories, 2 g fat (.5 g saturated fat), 55 mg cholesterol, 22 g protein, 8 g carbohydrate, 94 mg sodium

# SOLE WITH MACADAMIA BUTTER

Servings: 2

*Browned butter gilds fish fillets for a tasty finish.*

1½ tbs. butter or margarine
2 tbs. chopped macadamia nuts or
  sliced almonds

1 tsp. lemon juice
8 oz. sole or turbot fillets
salt and pepper to taste

Place butter and nuts in a small baking dish and microwave on High for 1 to 2 minutes or until bubbly and butter and nuts turn a pale golden color. Add lemon juice. Place fish in a baking dish, season with salt and pepper, and cover with waxed paper. Microwave on High for 2 minutes or until fish just turns opaque. Spoon browned nut butter over all and let stand 5 minutes.

*per serving*   239 calories, 16 g fat (7 g saturated fat), 78 mg cholesterol, 22 g protein, 1 g carbohydrate, 180 mg sodium

# TUNA IN A YOGURT CLOAK

Servings: 1 or 2

*The spark of mustard and herbs uplift this flavorful fish bake.*

4 oz. tuna, swordfish or halibut steak
1 tsp. Dijon mustard
2 tsp. dry white wine
2 tbs. *Yogurt Cheese*, page 17

1 tbs. chopped Italian parsley
2 tsp. julienned orange peel
½ tsp. fresh tarragon or ⅛ tsp. dried
1 orange slice, with peel on

Place fish on a baking dish. In a small bowl, mix together the mustard, wine, *Yogurt Cheese*, parsley, orange peel and tarragon. Spoon over top of fish. Cover lightly with waxed paper. Microwave on High for 1 minute or longer, until fish flakes with a fork. Let stand 5 minutes. Garnish with orange slice, slit half way to the center and twisted. Makes 1 serving.

For 2 servings, double ingredients and microwave on High for 2 to 2½ minutes or until fish flakes with a fork.

For conventional cooking, bake fish in a preheated 375° oven for 10 to 12 minutes or until cooked through.

*per serving*  240 calories, 7 g fat (2 g saturated fat), 48 mg cholesterol, 31 g protein, 10 g carbohydrate, 165 mg sodium

# WINTER FISH PLATTER DINNER

Servings: 1 or 2

*The winter roots show off in this attractive dinner plate that is aromatic with the licorice scent of fennel.*

4 oz. tuna or rockfish, cut into 1-inch chunks
1 tbs. lemon juice
½ tsp. fennel seeds
2 teaspoons lemon zest
2 tbs. chopped parsley
1 rutabaga, peeled and sliced or 1 large carrot, sliced on the diagonal

1 parsnip, peeled and sliced
4 stalks fennel, thinly sliced
4 Brussels sprouts, halved
1 green onion, chopped
salt and pepper to taste
¼ cup chicken stock
fennel weed for garnish

In a small bowl, toss fish with lemon juice and fennel seeds; add half the lemon zest and parsley; let stand a few minutes. On a microwaveable dinner plate, arrange overlapping slices of rutabaga in a semi-circle on one outer side of plate. Arrange parsnips slices on the opposite outer side. Place fennel in center and flank with Brussels sprouts; sprinkle with green onion and remaining lemon zest, parsley, salt and pepper. Pour over chicken stock and cover with vented plastic wrap. Microwave on High for 5 minutes. Place fish on fennel.

Cover with plastic wrap and microwave on High 1 to 1½ minutes or until fish is barely cooked through. Let stand 5 minutes. Garnish with a few wisps of fennel weed. Makes 1 serving.

For 2 servings, double the recipe and arrange 2 plates. Microwave them separately as per directions.

*per serving* 397 calories, 7 g fat (2 g saturated fat), 43 mg cholesterol, 34 g protein, 54 g carbohydrate, 486 mg sodium

# POULTRY ENTRÉES

# CHICKEN TARRAGON WITH MUSHROOMS

Servings: 1 or 2

*Dijon mustard and tarragon give a fast uplift to chicken.*

2 boneless chicken breasts, about 8 oz.
2 tsp. Dijon mustard
1 tsp. finely julienned lemon peel
2 tsp. chopped fresh tarragon
1 tbs. chopped Italian parsley

1 cup sliced mushrooms
salt and pepper to taste
2 tbs. dry white wine
2 tbs. grated Parmesan or Romano
  cheese

Arrange chicken in a pie plate with thickest portion toward outside. Mix together mustard, lemon peel, tarragon, and parsley; spread over chicken. Scatter mushrooms over chicken, season with salt and pepper, and drizzle with wine. Cover with waxed paper and microwave on High for 3 to 4 minutes or until chicken is no longer pink inside, rotating dish once. Sprinkle with Parmesan; let stand, covered, 2 minutes. Makes 2 servings.

For 1 serving, divide ingredients in half and microwave on High for about 2 minutes.

*per serving*   239 calories, 13 g fat (5 g saturated fat), 203 mg cholesterol, 78 g protein, 5 g carbohydrate, 537 mg sodium

# SAUSAGE AND APPLE PLATTER DINNER

Servings: 1 or 2

*Smoked and pre-cooked specialty sausages are becoming more available and are an ideal star for a flavor-packed entrée surrounded by eye-catching vegetables and a fruit accent, all microwaved together. In combination, the grouping cooks together uniformally, making a swift-to-prepare and neat-to-serve main dish.*

1 medium potato, sliced with peel on
1 medium carrot, peeled and
  diagonally sliced
4 inner stalks celery heart, about
  4 inches long
1 green onion, chopped
½ Granny Smith apple, cored and
  sliced, with peel on

1 tsp. fresh thyme or ¼ tsp. dried
salt and pepper to taste
¼ cup chicken stock
1 smoked chicken and apple sausage
  or other smoked sausage
Dijon mustard for accompaniment

On a microwaveable dinner plate, arrange overlapping slices of potato in a semi-circle on one outer side of plate. Arrange carrot slices on opposite outer side. Place celery in center, sprinkle with green onions, and arrange apple slices alongside celery. Season with thyme, salt and pepper. Pour chicken stock over all and cover with vented plastic wrap. Microwave on High for 5 minutes. Place sausage on the celery, cover with plastic wrap, and microwave on High 1 to 1½ minutes or until hot through. Let stand 5 minutes. Serve, accompanied by Dijon mustard. Makes 1 serving.

For 2 servings, double the recipe and arrange 2 plates. Microwave them separately as per directions.

*per serving* 646 calories, 25 g fat (8 g saturated fat), 114 mg cholesterol, 34 g protein, 76 g carbohydrate, 1781 mg sodium

# YAM AND SAUSAGE PLATTER DINNER     Servings: 1 or 2

*This flavor combo mingles mandarin orange segments and apropos vegetables with duck and turkey sausage for a stylish all-in-one entrée plate.*

1 small yam or sweet potato, peeled and sliced
1 medium carrot, peeled and diagonally sliced
¾ cup shredded red Swiss chard or red cabbage
1 shallot, chopped
1 tsp. fresh thyme or ¼ tsp. dried

salt and pepper to taste
¼ cup chicken stock
1 smoked duck and turkey sausage (4 - 5 oz.), or other smoked sausage
1 mandarin orange, peeled and segmented
Dijon mustard for accompaniment

On a microwaveable dinner plate, arrange overlapping slices of yam or sweet potato in a semicircle on one outer side of plate. Arrange carrot slices on opposite outer side. Place Swiss chard in the center, and sprinkle with shallot, thyme, salt and pepper. Pour chicken stock over all and cover with vented plastic wrap. Microwave on High for 5 minutes. Place sausage on Swiss chard, flank with mandarin orange segments, cover with plastic wrap, and microwave on

High 1 to 1½ minutes or until hot through. Let stand 5 minutes. Serve, accompanied by Dijon mustard. Makes 1 serving.

For 2 servings, double the recipe and arrange 2 plates. Microwave them separately as per directions.

**per serving**   526 calories, 17 g fat (5 g saturated fat), 76 mg cholesterol, 24 g protein, 73 g carbohydrate, 1349 mg sodium

# CHICKEN PACKETS WITH FENNEL

Servings: 1 or 2

*The bright licorice accent of fennel makes a bed with other vegetables for chicken cooked in a paper casing — an entrée surprise.*

1 tbs. olive oil
2 boneless skinless chicken breasts, about 8 oz.
2 tsp. Dijon mustard
1 stalk fennel, finely julienned
1 small carrot, finely julienned
1 leek (white part only), finely julienned
1 tbs. chopped Italian parsley
1 tsp. chopped fresh thyme or ¼ tsp. dried
salt and pepper to taste

Fold two 10- by 15-inch pieces of parchment paper in half crosswise; trim corners to form ovals. Open ovals and brush with oil, leaving a 1-inch border around each. For each serving, place 1 chicken breast in center of one end of each oval; spread with mustard and sprinkle with fennel, carrot, leeks, parsley, thyme, salt and pepper. Fold paper over chicken and crimp edges to seal. Pierce top to vent slightly. Arrange on a baking plate and microwave on High for 3 to 4 minutes or until chicken is no longer pink inside, rotating once. Let stand 2 minutes. Makes 2 servings.

For 1 serving, divide ingredients in half and microwave on High for 1½ to 2 minutes.

For conventional cooking, place chicken packets in a baking dish and bake in a preheated 375° oven for 15 to 20 minutes or until cooked through.

***per serving*** 285 calories, 11 g fat (2 g saturated fat), 97 mg cholesterol, 36 g protein, 9 g carbohydrate, 161 mg sodium

# CHICKEN WITH CHEESE AND SUN-DRIED TOMATOES

Servings: 2

*The interplay of sweet caramel-like sun-dried tomatoes, peppery watercress or arugula and creamy goat cheese punctuates this festive chicken dish.*

1 tbs. olive oil
1 tbs. dry white wine
1 tsp. chopped fresh tarragon or ¼ tsp. dried
¼ tsp. paprika
2 boneless skinned chicken breasts,

pounded ¼-inch thick (about 8 oz.)
4 oil-cured sun-dried tomatoes
1 oz. Boursin or chevre, cut into 2 slices
8 sprigs watercress or arugula

In a 9-inch pie plate, place oil, wine, tarragon and paprika. Microwave on High for 20 seconds, to heat through. Swish chicken in mixture, turning to coat each side. Cover loosely with waxed paper. Microwave on High 1 minute. Turn chicken over. Microwave on High 30 seconds to 1 minute longer or until chicken is cooked through. Top with sun-dried tomatoes and cheese. Cover loosely with waxed paper and microwave on high for 30 seconds to warm cheese.

Serve warm or chilled on a bed of watercress or arugula. Makes 2 servings.

For conventional cooking, turn chicken in the seasoning mixture in a baking dish and bake in a 375° oven for 15 minutes or until cooked through. Top with tomatoes and cheese; bake 2 minutes longer to heat through.

**per serving**   260 calories, 11 g fat (2 g saturated fat), 73 mg cholesterol, 29 g protein, 12 g carbohydrate, 92 mg sodium

# APRICOT-GLAZED CHICKEN

Servings: 2

*A quick last minute broiling gives this easy chicken entrée an appealing mahogany glaze.*

2 tsp. sweet hot mustard
2 tbs. apricot chutney
2 tsp. soy sauce
2 boneless, skinless chicken breasts,
  pounded to even thickness

salt and pepper to taste
1 orange, peeled and sliced
watercress for garnish

In a 9-inch pie plate, mix together mustard, chutney, and soy sauce. Turn chicken in mixture, coating all sides. Season with salt and pepper. Microwave on High for 3 to 4 minutes. If desired, slip under broiler on an oven-proof dish to glaze lightly. Serve garnished with orange slices and watercress.

*per serving*   261 calories, 4 g fat (1 g saturated fat), 96 mg cholesterol, 37 g protein, 18 g carbohydrate, 526 mg sodium

# HERB AND LEMON ZESTED
# TURKEY STRIPS

*An abundance of herbs, lemon zest, and Dijon mustard punctuates this turkey entrée. The juices are superb over hot couscous or brown rice, or accompany with* **Sliced Potatoes and Turnips with Rosemary,** *page 59.*

5 oz. turkey thigh meat, cut into strips
2 tsp. Dijon-style mustard
1 tsp. lemon juice
1½ tsp. julienned lemon zest

1 tbs. chopped parsley
1 green onion, chopped
1 tsp. fresh rosemary or thyme
1 small clove garlic, minced

Prepare turkey strips. In a 6-inch pie plate or ramekin, mix together mustard, lemon juice, lemon zest, parsley, onion, rosemary and garlic. Add turkey and turn to coat. Let marinate 30 minutes. Cover with vented plastic wrap and microwave on High for 1½ minutes or until meat loses its pink color. Let stand 5 minutes.

For conventional cooking, place turkey strips on a broiling rack, foil-lined if desired, and broil just until cooked through, about 4 minutes.

*per serving* 290 calories, 11 g fat (3 g saturated fat), 120 mg cholesterol, 42 g protein, 5 g carbohydrate, 249 mg sodium

# CHICKEN PLATTER DINNER: EAST MEETS WEST

Servings: 1 or 2

*The sweet tang of chutney permeates chicken in this colorful dinner plate.*

1 small yam, peeled and thinly sliced
1 head baby bok choy or a few leaves Swiss chard, coarsely chopped
¼ cup chicken stock
½ tsp. chopped ginger root
8 to 10 pea pods, ends removed
2 shiitake mushrooms or 2 button mushrooms, sliced
1 green onion, chopped
1 tsp. fresh thyme or ¼ tsp. dried
4 oz. boneless chicken breast, thinly sliced and fanned slightly
1 tsp. sweet hot mustard
2 tsp. chutney

On a microwaveable dinner plate, arrange yam on one side of plate. Arrange bok choy on opposite outer side. Mix chicken stock and chopped ginger; spoon over vegetables. Cover with vented plastic wrap and microwave on High 5 minutes. Place pea pods and mushrooms in center and sprinkle with green onions and thyme. Spread chicken with a mixture of mustard and chutney; place over pea pods and mushrooms. Cover with plastic wrap and microwave on High 2 minutes or until chicken is no longer pink. Let stand 5 minutes. Makes 1 serving.

For 2 servings, double the recipe and arrange 2 plates. Microwave them separately as per directions.

---

***per serving*** 576 calories, 6 g fat (1 g saturated fat), 96 mg cholesterol, 45 g protein, 89 g carbohydrate, 687 mg sodium

---

# SMOKED TURKEY PLATTER DINNER

Servings: 1 or 2

*During the holiday season, this colorful plateful is particularly welcome.*

½ cup diced butternut or Hubbard squash
1 carrot or parsnip, peeled and sliced diagonally
3 Brussels sprouts, halved
2 button mushrooms, sliced
1 green onion, chopped
1 tsp. fresh thyme or ¼ tsp. dried
¼ cup chicken stock
4 oz. cooked smoked turkey breast
3 tbs. cranberries

On a microwaveable dinner plate, arrange squash on one side of plate. Arrange carrot or parsnip slices on opposite outer side. Place Brussels sprouts and mushrooms in center; sprinkle with green onion, thyme, salt and pepper. Pour chicken stock over all and cover with vented plastic wrap. Microwave on High for 5 minutes. Place turkey on sprouts and mushrooms and scatter on the cranberries.

Cover with plastic wrap and microwave on High 1 to 1½ minutes or until hot through. Let stand 5 minutes. Makes 1 serving.

For 2 servings, double the recipe and arrange 2 plates. Microwave them separately as per directions.

***per serving*** 286 calories, 5 g fat (1 g saturated fat), 52 mg cholesterol, 29 g protein, 37 g carbohydrate, 1253 mg sodium

# TURKEY AND PAPAYA PACIFIC STYLE

Servings: 1 or 2

*Lively seasonings of chutney, sesame oil and ginger lend verve to strips of dark turkey meat to finish off with a refreshing accent of fruit. Besides papaya, mango, tangerines, or seedless grapes can stand in.*

8 oz. turkey thigh meat, cut in 1-inch strips
3 tbs. mango or apricot chutney
2 tbs. lime juice
1 tsp. soy sauce
1 tsp. sesame oil
1 clove garlic, minced
1 tsp. chopped ginger root
½ tsp. chopped lemon zest or lemon grass (optional)
rice for accompaniment
papaya, mango, or tangerine segments or grapes
watercress for garnish

Prepare turkey meat. In a 9-inch pie plate stir together chutney, lime juice, soy, sesame oil, garlic, ginger root and lemon zest or lemon grass. Add turkey and turn to coat. Let marinate half and hour or longer. Arrange turkey in a circle around the edge of the dish. Cover with waxed paper. Microwave on High for 3 minutes or until turkey loses its pink color. Let stand 5 minutes. Serve over hot rice and garnish with fruit and watercress. Makes 2 servings.

For 1 serving, divide ingredients in half and microwave 1½ to 2 minutes.

For conventional cooking, place marinated turkey strips on a broiling rack, foil-lined if desired, and broil until cooked through, about 4 to 5 minutes.

---

*per serving*  305 calories, 11 g fat, (3 g saturated fat), 81 mg cholesterol, 33 g protein, 18 g carbohydrate, 312 mg sodium

# TURKEY BREAST CORDON BLEU

Servings: 1 or 2

*A pinwheel of ham and Gruyére centers these neat turkey roll-ups. Serve warm or chilled for an elegant treat.*

⅓ cup fine dry bread crumbs
¼ tsp. dried thyme
dash freshly ground pepper
1 oz. or 4 thin slices Black Forest
 ham or prosciutto or boiled ham
8 oz. turkey scallopini, 4 slices
 pounded about ⅛ inch thick

2 tsp. Dijon mustard
1 oz. Gruyére, Jarlsberg or Swiss
 cheese
1 egg, lightly beaten
2 tsp. olive oil
Italian parsley and lemon wedges for
 garnish

In a 9-inch pie plate, combine bread crumbs, thyme and pepper; microwave on High for 1½ to 2 minutes or until toasted, stirring once or twice. Set aside. Place a slice of ham over each slice of turkey; spread mustard over ham. Cut cheese in slices and arrange on ham. Roll up and secure with a toothpick. Blend egg and olive oil together. Dip rolls in egg mixture and then in crumbs, coating all over. Arrange on a pie plate around the outer edge. Cover with waxed paper and microwave on High for 3 to 4 minutes, turning over and repositioning once, cooking until no longer pink inside. Let stand 2 minutes. Serve hot or cold, garnished with parsley and lemon wedges. Makes 2 servings.

For 1 serving, divide ingredients in half and microwave on High 1½ to 2 minutes or until cooked through.

Note: a cluster of red and gold cherry tomatoes, mushroom caps and marinated artichoke hearts makes a nice accompaniment when the rolls are served cold.

For conventional cooking, place pie plate of turkey rolls in a preheated 375° oven and bake for 15 to 20 minutes or until cooked through.

**per serving** 420 calories, 19 g fat (6 g saturated fat), 216 mg cholesterol, 47 g protein, 13 g carbohydrate, 535 mg sodium

# TURKEY AND PEPPERS ORANGERIE

Servings: 1 or 2

*Red and gold pepper strips and green onions lend a festive color palette to this zestful turkey entrée. The thigh meat is easily sliced into strips and stays particularly moist in the microwave.*

5 oz. turkey thigh strips, about ½ by 2 inches and ¼ -inch thick
1 tsp. Dijon mustard
2 tsp. orange marmalade
¼ tsp. soy sauce
1 green onion, chopped
1 tsp. julienned orange peel
⅓ cup julienned red or gold pepper strips or a mixture of both
hot couscous, brown rice, or wild rice for accompaniment
1 tsp. chopped Italian parsley

Prepare turkey strips. In a small baking dish, stir together mustard, marmalade, soy sauce, onion, and orange peel. Add turkey strips and turn to coat. Lay them out in a single layer. Scatter pepper strips over turkey. Cover with waxed paper. Microwave on High for 1½ to 2 minutes or until almost cooked through. Let stand 3 to 4 minutes. Serve alongside couscous or rice and sprinkle with parsley. Makes 1 serving.

For 2 servings, double ingredients and microwave on High for about 4 minutes.

For conventional cooking, bake in a preheated 375° oven for 10 to 15 minutes or until turkey is cooked through.

*per serving*  335 calories, 11 g fat (3 g saturated fat), 120 mg cholesterol, 42 g protein, 17 g carbohydrate, 271 mg sodium

# GROUND TURKEY PIZZABURGER

Servings: 1 or 2

*A ground turkey patty forms a succulent base for pizza toppings.*

¼ lb. ground turkey
1½ tbs. seasoned tomato sauce
2 green onions, sliced

4 mushrooms, sliced
¼ tsp. dried oregano
2 tbs. shredded Romano cheese

Pat turkey out into a 6-inch round, making a slight rim. Place on a baking dish or pie pan. Spread with tomato sauce. Sprinkle with onions, mushrooms, oregano and cheese. Bake in a 425° oven for 10 to 12 minutes or until cooked through. Makes 1 serving.

For 2 servings, double the ingredients and prepare 2 pizzaburgers.

*per serving*  221 calories, 9 g fat (4 g saturated fat), 96 mg cholesterol, 38 g protein, 7 g carbohydrate, 350 mg sodium

# GRILLED TURKEY PATTIES
# WITH HERBS

16 small patties

*These little turkey patties are so flavorful chilled that you'll want to make a double batch to have some left over for lunch.*

1 lb. ground turkey
1 egg white
¼ cup dry red wine
2 cloves garlic, minced
salt and pepper to taste
¼ tsp. ground allspice or cinnamon

2 tbs. chopped parsley
1 tsp. fresh oregano or ¼ tsp. dried
1 tbs. balsamic vinegar
2 tsp. Dijon mustard
1 tsp. olive oil

In a bowl, mix together ground turkey, egg white, wine, garlic, salt, pepper, allspice, parsley and oregano. With a very small ice cream scoop or two spoons, scoop out meat mixture into small balls and drop it on a sheet of foil on a broiling pan, making about 16 patties. Flatten slightly. Broil about 3 minutes on each side, turning once. Mix together vinegar, mustard and olive oil; brush over patties. Broil a minute longer to glaze.

*per 4-pattie serving*  291 calories, 17 g fat (4 g saturated fat), 78 mg cholesterol, 29 g protein, 2 g carbohydrate, 142 mg sodium

# TURKEY ROLLS VERONIQUE

Servings: 1 or 2

*Thinly sliced turkey breast makes neat compact rolls to glaze with a hot grape sauce.*

8 oz. turkey breast fillet, thinly sliced
1 tsp. chopped tarragon or thyme or ¼ tsp. dried
1 tsp. olive oil
1 tbs. orange marmalade
1 tbs. sweet hot mustard
2 tbs. dry white wine
1 tbs. lemon juice
salt, pepper, and paprika to taste
1 cup seedless green or red grapes, halved
orange slices and parsley sprigs or watercress for garnish

Pound turkey slices to an even thickness. Sprinkle with tarragon and roll up slices. In a pie plate combine oil, marmalade, mustard, wine and lemon juice. Microwave on High 30 seconds to 1 minute to heat through. Turn turkey rolls in mixture and arrange around outer edge of dish. Sprinkle with salt, pepper and paprika to taste. Cover with waxed paper and microwave on High for 3 to 4 minutes or until turkey loses its pink color inside. Add grapes and microwave on High 30 seconds longer or until heated through. Let stand 2 minutes. Garnish with orange slices and parsley or watercress sprigs.

For 1 serving, divide ingredients in half and microwave on High for 1 to 2 minutes or until cooked through.

**per serving**   281 calories, 4 g fat (1 g saturated fat), 97 mg cholesterol, 36 g protein, 23 g carbohydrate, 166 mg sodium

# TURKEY TANDOORI

*Boneless turkey strips bathe in a spicy yogurt sauce for this Indian-style entrée. Accompany with brown rice tossed with pistachios for a chewy partner.*

8 oz. turkey breast, cut in 1½ by
  ½-inch strips
1 tbs. lemon juice
1½ tsp. chopped ginger root
¼ tsp. turmeric
¼ tsp. paprika

¼ tsp. ground coriander
dash cinnamon, allspice and cayenne
1 clove garlic, minced
¼ cup yogurt
cilantro sprigs for garnish

Prepare turkey breast in even strips. In a bowl, mix together lemon juice, ginger root, turmeric, paprika, coriander, cinnamon, allspice, cayenne, garlic and yogurt. Add turkey pieces and turn to coat. Cover and refrigerate for 8 hours or overnight, turning several times. Place in a 9-inch pie plate around the outer edge. Cover with waxed paper and microwave on High for 3 to 4 minutes or until no longer pink. Serve warm or chilled, garnished heavily with cilantro.

For conventional cooking, thread marinated turkey cubes on 2 skewers. Place on a broiling rack and broil 6 to 8 minutes, or until cooked through.

*per serving*   185 calories, 2 g fat (1 g saturated fat), 101 mg cholesterol, 36 g protein, 3 g carbohydrate, 77 mg sodium

# DESSERTS

# RAISIN-STUFFED BAKED APPLES

Servings: 1 or 2

*Golden raisins and a splash of Calvados or Cognac uplift homey baked apples.*

2 Granny Smith or Golden Delicious
 apples
2 tbs. golden raisins

1 tbs. honey or brown sugar
2 tsp. butter
1½ tbs. Calvados or Cognac

Remove core of each apple to ½ inch of bottom; prick skin all over. Place apples in a 9-inch pie plate or individual small pie plates. Into the center of each apple divide raisins, honey, butter and Calvados. Cover with vented plastic wrap and microwave on High for 4 to 5 minutes or until apples are tender, rotating halfway through. Makes 2 servings.

For 1 serving, divide ingredients in half and microwave on High for 2 to 3 minutes or until apples are tender.

For conventional cooking, bake in a 375° oven for 40 to 45 minutes or until apples are tender.

*per serving*  262 calories, 12 g fat (7 g saturated fat), 31 mg cholesterol, 1 g protein, 39 g carbohydrate, 121 mg sodium

# BANANAS FLAMBÉ

*Rum, Cognac or Amaretto can flame hot bananas.*

1/4 orange juice
2 tbs. brown sugar
1 tsp. lemon juice
dash cinnamon or allspice

2 bananas, peeled and cut in half
  lengthwise
2 tbs. rum, Cognac or Amaretto

In a 9-inch pie plate, combine orange juice, brown sugar, lemon juice and cinnamon. Microwave on High for 1 minute; stir. Place bananas in sauce, turning them to coat and placing them flat sides up. Cover with waxed paper and microwave on High for 1 to 1½ minutes or until heated through. Remove from microwave. Pour liqueur into a 1-cup glass measure and microwave on High for 15 seconds. Pour liqueur over bananas and ignite with a match. Makes 2 servings.

For 1 serving, divide ingredients and timing in half.

---

***per serving***   204 calories, 1 g fat (0 g saturated fat), 0 mg cholesterol, 1 g protein, 49 g carbohydrate, 6 mg sodium

# CARAMELIZED ORANGE SLICES

Servings: 2

*An orange liqueur-spiked caramel sauce gilds tangy sweet orange slices.*

2 large seedless oranges
¼ cup granulated sugar
2 tbs. orange juice
1 tbs. orange liqueur
1 tbs. chopped roasted pistachios or toasted slivered almonds

Peel oranges and thinly slice. Arrange on dessert plates in a semicircle. Place sugar and orange juice in a microwaveable baking dish. Microwave uncovered on High for 2 minutes or until golden. Immediately pour over orange slices and drizzle with liqueur. Sprinkle with nuts.

*per serving* 201 calories, 2 g fat (0 g saturated fat), 0 mg cholesterol, 2 g protein, 45 g carbohydrate, 2 mg sodium

# CHOCOLATE-DIPPED STRAWBERRIES

Servings: 2

*Either dark or white chocolate can glaze juicy berries for a special treat.*

2 oz. (1/3 cup) semisweet or white chocolate pieces
2 tsp. unsalted butter
1 cup strawberries with hulls and preferably stems, chilled

Place chocolate in a circle in a 9-inch pie plate, adding butter to center. Cook on Medium for 1 minute; stir to blend. Cook on Medium 30 seconds longer or until melted. Holding each berry by the hull, dip halfway into chocolate, twirling to coat. Place hull side down on a waxed paper-lined baking sheet. Refrigerate 15 minutes to firm up.

***per serving*** 267 calories, 22 g fat (13 g saturated fat), 31 mg cholesterol, 2 g protein, 21 g carbohydrate, 6 mg sodium

## Variations: Chocolate-dipped Apricots or Tangerines

Substitute 3/4 cup dried apricots for the strawberries, coating half of each round, or 1 cup tangerine segments for the strawberries, coating half of each segment.

# SUMMER FRUIT COMPOTE

*As this compote chills, the berries exude their colorful juices, turning the citrus syrup scarlet.*

¼ cup orange juice
2 tbs. lime juice
½ tsp. each grated orange and lime
  peel
3 tbs. sugar
1 cup watermelon balls

¾ cup hulled halved strawberries
⅓ cup raspberries
¾ cup seedless grapes
3 tbs. blueberries (optional)
2 mint sprigs

In a 1-cup glass measure, combine orange juice, lime juice, orange peel, lime peel, and sugar. Cover with vented plastic wrap and microwave on High for 2 minutes or until sugar is dissolved. Let cool and chill. In a bowl, place melon, strawberries, raspberries, grapes and blueberries. Pour citrus juices over fruit. Cover and chill 3 hours or longer, stirring gently once or twice. Serve in bowls garnished with mint sprigs.

*per serving*   144 calories, 1 g fat (0 g saturated fat), 0 mg cholesterol, 1 g protein, 36 g carbohydrate, 3 mg sodium

# FRUIT PLATE WITH HONEYED PISTACHIOS

*This colorful fruit plate can change with the seasons.*

2 tbs. coarsely chopped pistachios or slivered or sliced almonds
1 tsp. honey
1 kiwi fruit

1 cup strawberries
½ cup blueberries or raspberries
1½ tbs. orange liqueur or kirsch

Place nuts and honey in a lightly buttered small custard cup or baking dish. Microwave uncovered on High for 1½ to 2 minutes or until nuts are toasted and honey is caramelized. Peel and slice kiwi fruit and arrange slices overlapping on 2 dessert plates. Place strawberries alongside and scatter blueberries or raspberries over fruits. Spoon liqueur over all and sprinkle with nuts.

*per serving*   151 calories, 5 g fat (.5 g saturated fat), 0 mg cholesterol, 2 g protein, 25 g carbohydrate, 68 mg sodium

## Variation
For fruits use 2 sliced nectarines and ½ cup raspberries with orange liqueur.

# GINGERED BAKED PAPAYA

*These hot papaya boats make a fun meat, poultry or fish accompaniment or a low calorie healthful dessert.*

1 small papaya, halved and seeded
1 tbs. honey
1 tbs. lime juice

1 tsp. chopped fresh ginger root
2 lime wedges for garnish
edible flowers for garnish

Place papaya halves cut side up in a 9-inch pie plate. Divide honey, lime juice and ginger root in the center of each. Cover with waxed paper and microwave on High for 2 to 3 minutes or until heated through. Serve on plates garnished with lime wedges and flowers.

For conventional cooking, bake in a preheated 375° oven for 10 to 15 minutes or until heated through.

*per serving* 98 calories, 0 g fat (0 g saturated fat), 0 mg cholesterol, 1 g protein, 25 g carbohydrate, 5 mg sodium

# ALMOND-COATED PEACHES FLAMBÉ

Servings: 2

*Peaches are pretty sealed with a rosy currant glaze and an almond coating. The white Babcock variety is a juicy, elegant peach to use.*

2 peaches
2 tbs. currant jelly
2 tbs. finely chopped toasted blanched almonds
2 tbs. dark rum, Cognac or Amaretto

Dip peaches in boiling water for 30 seconds, then dip in cold water and slip off skins. Place jelly in a 9-inch pie plate and microwave on High for 30 seconds or until melted. Roll peaches in jelly and sprinkle with almonds, coating the surface. Microwave rum in a small custard cup on High for 15 seconds or until hot. Ignite 1 tablespoon on a spoon and spoon flaming over peaches. Gradually pour over remaining rum.

---

**per serving**   169 calories, 4 g fat (0 g saturated fat), 0 mg cholesterol, 2 g protein, 29 g carbohydrate, 5 mg sodium

# PINEAPPLE RINGS JAMAICAN

*Rum-imbued pineapple rings are luscious with frosty frozen yogurt or sorbet.*

2 tsp. butter or margarine
2 fresh pineapple slices, about ½-inch thick
2 tbs. maple syrup or brown sugar
1 tbs. rum, Amaretto, or orange liqueur

frozen yogurt in vanilla, peach or strawberry flavors; fruit sorbet; or toasted almond or coffee ice cream
mint sprigs for garnish

Place butter in a 9-inch pie plate and microwave on High for 20 seconds to melt. Place pineapple slices in melted butter, turning to coat both sides. Drizzle with maple syrup and rum. Cover with waxed paper and microwave on High for 1 minute. Turn slices over and cook 30 seconds longer or until hot through. Place on dessert plates, spoon juices over pineapple and top with a scoop of frozen yogurt. Garnish with a mint sprig. Makes 2 servings.

For 1 serving, divide ingredients and timing in half.

***per serving***  244 calories, 5 g fat (3 g saturated fat), 15 mg cholesterol, 3 g protein, 45 g carbohydrate, 73 mg sodium

# WINE POACHED PEARS

Servings: 2

*Anjou or Bosc pears are excellent in this warm spicy fruit bowl. Accompany with yogurt or frozen yogurt.*

1 tbs. lemon juice
1 tbs. honey
¼ cup sweet white wine, late harvest
  wine or Port
dash cinnamon and nutmeg

2 large firm pears
half lemon
yogurt or frozen yogurt or ice cream
  for accompaniment

In a 9-inch pie plate, combine lemon juice, honey, wine, cinnamon and nutmeg. Halve and core pears; rub with a cut lemon half. Arrange pears in pie plate cut side down in a circle with thick ends toward outside. Cover with vented plastic wrap and microwave on High for 1 to 1½ minutes or until pears are almost tender. Spoon poaching liquid over pears and microwave 30 seconds longer, or until just tender. Spoon pears into dessert bowls. Microwave juices on High 1 to 2 minutes longer, or until bubbly and slightly reduced. Spoon over pears. Serve warm, at room temperature, or chilled with yogurt or frozen yogurt.

*per serving*   229 calories, 2 g fat (1 g saturated fat), 5 mg cholesterol, 3 g protein, 47 g carbohydrate, 32 mg sodium

# APPLE OATMEAL CRISP

*A crunchy caramelized topping gilds apple slices in minutes for a fast dessert.*

2 tbs. oatmeal
1 tbs. unbleached or wholewheat flour
4 tsp. brown sugar, packed
2 tsp. butter or margarine
1 cup peeled, sliced apples (about 1 medium apple)
dash cinnamon
frozen vanilla yogurt (optional)

In a custard cup, place oatmeal, flour, sugar, and butter; mix with fingers until crumbly. Microwave on High for 1 minute. Spread apples in a shallow 6-inch ramekin or baking dish and sprinkle with cinnamon. Sprinkle with oatmeal topping. Microwave on High for 3 minutes or until topping is golden and apples are tender. Let stand for 5 minutes. Serve warm plain or top with frozen vanilla yogurt. Makes 1 serving.

For 2 servings, double ingredients and place in 2 ramekins; microwave about 4 minutes or until tender.

## Variations

### Nectarine and Blueberry Crisp
Substitute ¾ cup sliced nectarines and ¼ cup blueberries for the apples. Replace cinnamon with grated nutmeg.

### Pear and Cranberry Crisp
Substitute ¾ cup peeled, sliced pears and ¼ cup cranberries for the apples.

### Plum Crisp
Substitute 1 cup quartered or sliced plums for the apples. Replace cinnamon with 1 tsp. chopped preserved ginger, tossed with the fruit.

---

*per serving Apple Oatmeal Crisp*   379 calories, 24 g fat (14 g saturated fat), 62 mg cholesterol, 2 g protein, 43 g carbohydrate, 288 mg sodium

---

# BUTTERSCOTCH SAUCE

*This golden sauce makes a wonderful sundae topping. Reheat it on Medium for a minute or two the second time around.*

½ cup sugar
2 tbs. light corn syrup
2 tsp. hot water
2 tbs. butter or margarine
¼ cup half-and-half

In a 1-quart glass measure, combine sugar, corn syrup and water. Cover tightly with plastic wrap and microwave on Medium for 1 minute or until sugar is dissolved. Stir well, uncover and microwave on High 2 to 3 minutes longer or until mixture reaches a light golden color, stirring once. Cut butter into pieces and add to warm mixture, stirring until melted. Stir in half-and-half. Cook on High for 1 minute or until blended. Let stand a few minutes before serving.

---

***per tablespoon***   98 calories, 3 g fat (2 g saturated fat), 7mg cholesterol, 0 g protein, 19 g carbohydrate, 24 mg sodium

---

# CHOCOLATE LEAVES

2 leaves

*Decorative chocolate leaves are quite easy to make for an eye-catching edible container for ice cream or fresh fruit. Radicchio or small cabbage leaves work well.*

2 oz. semisweet chocolate pieces
2 attractive radicchio or cabbage leaves, about 4 to 5 inches in diameter

Place chocolate around outer rim of a microwaveable cereal bowl. Microwave on Medium for 1 to 2 minutes or until chocolate is soft enough to spread, stirring once or twice. Take a small spatula and spread chocolate as evenly as possible on top side of leaf, being careful not to leave any holes. Repeat with second leaf. Place in freezer for 10 to 15 minutes to firm up. When chocolate is solid, carefully pull off leaves. Return chocolate to a closed container and refrigerate until ready to use. Fill leaves with ice cream or fruit berries or both. Makes 2 chocolate leaves.

*per leaf*   152 calories, 10 g fat (6 g saturated fat), 0 mg cholesterol, 2 g protein, 18 g carbohydrate, 10 mg sodium

# CHOCOLATE SUNDAE SAUCE

Servings: 2

*This is a wonderful sauce on ice cream as it sets up into a caramel-like syrup when it hits the frosty scoops. It also lends itself to many versatile variations. Make in a larger quantity if desired, and then reheat. Remember chocolate melts at about 90°, so it is important to not overheat it.*

2 oz. semisweet chocolate (or ⅓ cup chocolate chips)
2 tbs. light corn syrup
1½ tbs. strong coffee

In a 1-cup glass measure, place chocolate, corn syrup and coffee. Heat in a microwave uncovered on Medium for 1 minute, stirring once or twice, or until melted and smoothly blended.

***per serving*** 209 calories, 10 g fat (6 g saturated fat), 0 mg cholesterol, 2 g protein, 33 g carbohydrate, 19 mg sodium

# SERVING IDEAS

## Pears Helene
Halve, core and thinly slice 1 Comice or Anjou pear. Divide slices into 2 dessert bowls. Add a scoop of vanilla or toasted almond ice cream to each bowl and top with hot *Chocolate Sundae Sauce*. Makes 2 servings.

## Blueberry Coffee Sundaes
Place a scoop of coffee ice cream in each of 2 dessert bowls and scatter ¼ cup blueberries over each. Top with hot *Chocolate Sundae Sauce*. Makes 2 servings.

## Marron Chocolate Sundaes
Place a scoop of vanilla bean ice cream in each of 2 dessert bowls and spoon 3 tbs. marron glace with syrup over each one. Top with *Chocolate Sundae Sauce*. Makes 2 servings.

## Raspberry Chocolate Sundaes
Place a scoop of vanilla ice cream in each of two dessert bowls and scatter ¼ cup raspberries over each. Top with *Chocolate Sundae Sauce*. Makes 2 servings.

# PRALINE POWDER

*This versatile dessert condiment can top fresh fruit, such as sliced pineapple, nectarines. oranges or berries or shower it over an ice cream sundae or use as a garnish on whipped cream.*

½ cup sugar
3 tbs. water
½ cup toasted blanched almonds, hazelnuts or pecans

Combine sugar and water in a 1-quart glass measure. Cover tightly with plastic wrap and microwave on High about 3 to 4 minutes or until syrup is golden, watching carefully. Add nuts, stir to coat using an oiled spatula and pour out on an oiled baking sheet. Let cool. When hard, break praline into small pieces. Place in a food processor or blender or process to a fine powder. Store in an airtight container.

**per tablespoon**  100 calories, 5 g fat (.5 g saturated fat), 0 mg cholesterol, 2 g protein, 14 g carbohydrate, 1 mg sodium

# INDEX